BUSES ANNUAL 1988

£6.00

Below:

Greater Manchester 1752, a Northern Counties-bodied Dennis Domino, loads at Piccadilly Station, Manchester, on the Centreline service to Victoria Station. The Domino was developed from the double-deck Dominator specifically for this service. *Stewart J. Brown*

BUSES ANNUAL 1988

Edited by STEWART J. BROWN

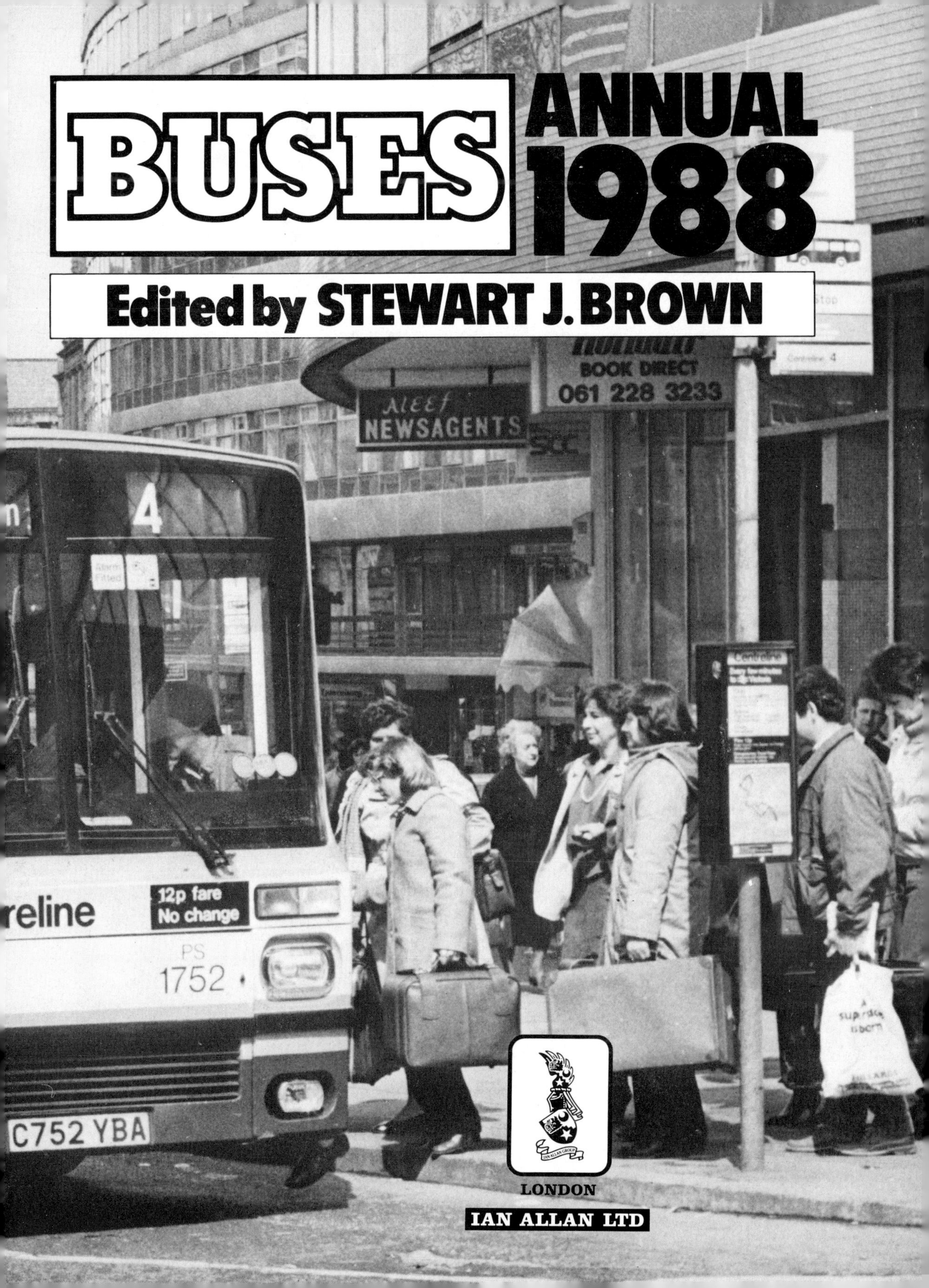

LONDON

IAN ALLAN LTD

Contents

Front cover:
The tendering of routes by London Regional Transport has added splashes of colour to various parts of the capital and has meant in many cases the reintroduction of previously withdrawn DMS-type Fleetlines with independent operators. Limebourne's Cityrama operation has so far won contracts for two routes, one of which is the 200, Raynes Park-Streatham Hill. Cityrama took over its operation of 22 March 1986 and former DM1811 is seen on the route a few weeks later. *R. Hefford*

Introduction		5
What did you do on D-day, Daddy?	*Stephen Morris*	6
Variety at Ipswich	*Ian Cowley*	11
Confessions of an ageing enthusiast	*Gavin Booth*	14
Looking back	*Roy Marshall*	20
Routemasters in Scotland	*Ian Train*	28
End of an era	*Stewart J. Brown*	34
Bristol's Lodekka	*Martin Curtis*	45
Tender stakes tame the wayward child	*Alan Millar*	54
Down under	*John Aldridge*	62
The end of the road	*Roger Kaye*	69
The Super National programme	*Mike Cornish*	72
After the Atlantean	*John Burnett*	78
The *Buses Annual* 1988 quiz		82
Cornwall independents before deregulation	*Graham Wise*	84
Twixt Tyne and Wear	*Kevin Lane*	92
Topless buses	*John Milnes*	96
On hire to National	*Geoff Mills*	99

First published 1987

ISBN 0 7110 1696 8

Published by Ian Allan Ltd, Shepperton, Surrey; and printed by Ian Allan Printing Ltd at their works at Coombelands in Runnymede, England

The ones that got away	*Michael Dryhurst*	102
Over and under	*Simon Butler*	110
All change on the long island	*Sandy Macdonald*	113
North Western 'deckers	*Reg Wilson*	119
Channel Isle	*Michael Fowler*	122
Scotland in winter	*Robert Grieves*	126

Introduction

Many of the readers of *Buses Annual* are also readers of its monthly counterpart, *Buses*, and among the contributors to this year's annual they will find two familiar names — Stephen Morris, editor of *Buses*, and Sandy Macdonald, the regular Scottish columnist. Both consider territories familiar to them — Surrey and Scotland respectively. And while Stephen Morris takes a look at one of the biggest events of the decade — deregulation of local bus services in 1986 — other contributors recall less stormy days. Graham Wise takes a look at rural Cornwall in the early 1980s, while Martin Curtis relates the story of a bus which was familiar to all British enthusiasts for a quarter of a century from the mid-1950s to the late 1970s — the Bristol Lodekka.

Other makes which receive attention in this year's *Annual* are Bedford, now no longer with us as a bus and coach builder, and some special Leyland Nationals, in a feature written by Mike Cornish, a man who was closely involved in their development.

London escaped deregulation in 1986 and Alan Millar examines some of the effects of London Regional Transport's tendering procedures, while for those with cosmopolitan tastes John Aldridge describes some of the bus interests which he found on a visit to Australia. And if your interest is in old vehicles then Michael Dryhurst's thoughts on buses which should have been preserved but weren't is the article for you.

Add to all this photo-features by some of the best bus photographers around and you have a fair idea of what the 1988 *Buses Annual* is all about.

I hope you enjoy it!

Stewart J. Brown

Withnell

Stephen Morris

What did you do on D-day, Daddy?

Deregulated bus services are now a fact of life — indeed it is often hard to remember what all the fuss was about in the run-up to deregulation. *Buses* editor Stephen Morris casts his mind back to the fateful day.

I must confess I would have liked to have been in Manchester to observe the full effects of the first Monday of deregulation. Admittedly I usually do like to be in Manchester anyway, but I was intrigued by the thought of Ribble working within the confines of the city on local services, and curious as to what Walls Coaches' W42 service would turn out to be like — something I had wondered ever since I first saw the registration for it in those bumper issues of *Notices & Proceedings* the previous March. But 'twas not to be. In fixing a date for D-day Nicholas Ridley, then Transport Secretary, might just have spared a thought for a poor editor trying to cope with deregulation at the same time as putting a Motor Show issue to bed. So D-day and thereabout had to be spent nowhere more exciting than northwest Surrey, not too far away from an editorial desk which was even more hectic and chaotic than usual.

D-day itself was bound to be rather a damp squib locally. It was, of course, a Sunday and Sunday buses locally are few and far between. The need for a grand send-off at Heathrow for a friend going abroad reduced bus-watching opportunities further — but proved useful, in that the excellent travel centre under the central bus station at the airport was able to provide a local timetable booklet; every available copy in Shepperton had already been snapped up before I got there.

But we did manage a valedictory journey on a London Buses 218 the previous day. The 218, and its predecessors, had been trundling its slightly circuitous way between Staines and Kingston for many a year, and was one of the last routes to be operated by red RFs, which in latter days had looked increasingly quaint — especially when London Country replaced virtually everything in the Staines area with new Leyland Nationals and AEC Reliances around 1977. In more recent times Leyland Nationals from Norbiton garage had been the order of the day. They were usually beautifully turned out; seldom would one be seen with paintwork looking scruffy or with a dirty interior. Sadly their appearance was seldom matched by service reliability though. Staines and environs had steadily become a far-flung outpost of the red bus empire, and around Shepperton and Walton-on-Thames the breed had become very rare, with steady retrenchment in favour of green London Country buses — and one or two independents, such as the late, lamented Ben Stanley. The 218 then was

Left:
A Thandi Coaches Volvo with Duple Dominant body loading at Heathrow's central bus station at the start of deregulated operation. *S. C. Morris*

Left:
Had he been in Manchester on the day after D-day, Stephen Morris could have seen ex-Greater Manchester Daimler Fleetlines smartly repainted in Walls' green and white livery — and with their identities obscured by personalised registrations. *Stewart J. Brown*

very much a last bastion — and reliability certainly seemed to suffer as a result.

In and around Shepperton nearly everyone has a car, if not two or more. Most teenagers seem either to have a motorcycle (what a shock they would get if the local constabulary ever took it upon themselves to enforce noise regulations) or to be learning to drive. If you ever happened to mention to anyone you were planning to go somewhere by bus, this revelation was usually received with a mixture of shock and pity; 'Oh you can't do *that*; why don't you borrow our car?' Not a promising environment for commercial bus operation. Who on earth would be daft enough to register something like the 218 as commercial?

In the event, two operators were. London Buses took the opportunity to halve the service to every hour. But London Country, not an operator without a good bit of commercial nonce, also registered a similar service, the 427, every half hour. In the event, London Buses decided to let London Country get on with the job, and quietly withdrew from the fray, enabling London Country to pick up the 218 number. Do you remember a time when all London Country routes began with a 3, 4, 7 or 8? And so it was that my wife and I went and shivered at the bus stop for a last ride on a red 218 from Shepperton to the local teeming metropolis of Staines.

Now in the days when London Country (then in one piece, not four) used numbers beginning with 3, 4, 7 or 8, London Transport drivers were never sent out without a long session of route-learning behind them. But when eventually a red LS charged round the corner at the top of the road at quite a jaunty angle, and over 20 minutes late, it seemed this was no longer the case. Now if the old adage about policemen looking young holds true for bus drivers, I must be pushing 102. (I'm not, incidentally). My request for two returns to Staines was met by much fumbling with a faretable, before the youthful driver admitted he had no idea where he was anyway! Eventually we got sorted out, but were rather disconcerted by the fact that the driver had with him an even more youthful friend acting as navigator, armed with no more sophisticated an aid than a Londonwide Bus Map! Quite why a driver who had obviously never been anywhere near the route before should be sent out on its last day, I know not; obviously somebody at Norbiton felt that no bus driver's education was complete without a turn on the 218! All credit to the lad with the bus map; we made it to Staines without major mishap, though I still like to speculate what might have happened when we came close to turning up a fairly narrow road that finishes in a dead end in mistake for the main road to Laleham! The LS too registered its discontent at its final spell on the 218 by refusing to select a gear from time to time, but never mind, we got there. But we succumbed to a lift home with a pitying and shocked friend whom we met in Staines; at least LBL had gained a little revenue from our return tickets. Thus ended red bus operation of the 218, and 56 years of regulation.

D-day itself, then, saw this writer doing not a lot of bus riding, although there was at least the opportunity to observe the odd green bus on the 218's hourly Sunday service and to regret the passing of London Buses' comprehensive blind display in favour of a terse 'Staines' or 'Kingston' as appropriate, sometimes in Green Line style black-on-yellow. But dull though the Shepperton area may be in bus terms — with the exception of Golden Miller's four-times daily service 602 to Feltham which can be relied upon to produce one or other of the smart Caetano Stagecoach-bodied Volvo B10Ms — deregulation at least gave rise to some interest and on the first Monday the services to Heathrow Airport were an obvious starting point. Shepperton, despite its proximity to the airport, hasn't had a service to Heathrow for very long. Prior to the introduction of London Country services 455 and 456, journeys by bus to and from the airport were a protracted affair. Given a good, following wind and favourable connections the journey could take an hour, though on

Left:
The 218 in the last summer of London Buses' operation. A Leyland National loads at Thorpe Park, Chertsey. *John Marsh*

one occasion I remember the journey taking 2¾ hours — and having to walk the last 3½ miles or so. The irony of this was enhanced by the fact I had arrived at Heathrow about 90min after leaving Van Hool's factory near Antwerp! A local estate agent claims that Shepperton is 15min from Heathrow — one day I will challenge them to get me there in that time — legally!

The introduction of the 455 and 456 was greatly appreciated but, judging by the loadings, obviously not by many of the local populace, and even at about 08.00 on a weekday it was a rare event to see more than half-a-dozen passengers on board. Not surprisingly no one registered them for commercial operation. But Surrey County Council saw the value of them, and out they went to tender, albeit with some truncation to the 456. When Surrey published its first tendering results, the 455 and 456 were, ominously, 'deferred'. But it transpired that the reason for the deferment was that the potentially successful bidder was a bit of an outsider, Warley (West Midlands)-based Thandi coaches. Thandi had no local service experience, but operated express services from Southall, where it had an operating base, to various points in the East and West Midlands and Yorkshire. Surrey therefore wished to assure itself that the company could operate these local services adequately and also that it would have suitable vehicles. Leyland Nationals were promised, and Mr Thandi himself even appeared on television with an ex-Greater Manchester National in evidence. Greater Manchester had, until a matter of weeks before D-day, refused to sell withdrawn vehicles for further service — as had a number of other public-sector operators. However, a shortage of ready cash for Greater Manchester Buses Ltd (and, one gathers, a little Governmental persuasion) meant that about 400 orange double-deckers and 100 Leyland Nationals adorned in similar hue suddenly appeared on the second-hand market. Good news for independents, though less so for hard-pressed manufacturers. But the late arrival of such vehicles on to the market made it difficult for them to be prepared for service in time for D-day, with the result that during the week leading up to deregulation Thandi's slightly shabby-looking Volvo coaches were observed on route-learning duties.

Monday 27 October dawned cold, grey and very wet. But nonetheless I had worked out an itinerary, using the local Surrey-produced timetable. Taking things a stage further from the old order of route-numbers, all Surrey contracted services were identified by a 5XX number, so 455 and 456 had become 555 and 556 respectively. The plan was to catch the 08.02 555 from Shepperton to Heathrow, the 09.20 from Heathrow to Walton-on-Thames, then sample a new delight, London Country South West 567, running by a roundabout route from Walton to Staines, returning to Shepperton by a green 218. I suppose I should have realised that part of the premise of the 1985 Act was to remove bus services from the hands of planners — and even planning by passengers was apparently now taboo! I arrived at the bus stop in reasonable time for the 555, and was a little disconcerted at seeing a Thandi coach heading towards Heathrow along another road, on the route of the 556, which should have gone half-an-hour earlier. Had the 555 driver, on his first day, got lost? No, perhaps it was a private hire, or some new commuter route which had somehow escaped my attention. By 08.15 I was less sure. And by 08.30, as the rainwater seeped through my shoes my fears were confirmed — deregulation cold feet had definitely set in!

But at 08.40, a Plaxton-bodied V-registered Volvo B58 pulled up with a disconcerting squeal of brakes. Its Bristol dome proclaimed 'Express', its side windows sported all sorts of exotic destinations — Birmingham, Wolverhampton, Leicester, Sheffield etc. But a paper sticker in the windscreen did state 555, so I boarded. Inside the coach sported all sorts of luxuries seldom to be found in a London Country Leyland National, like a drinks servery, a toilet and a TV monitor, plus curtains to the windows. None of the sophisticated bolt-on goodies was in operation, though, but the TV monitor, by the entrance, did make its presence felt by conspiring to clout just about every passenger on the head as they paid the driver, who issued tickets from an ancient Almex. As I boarded (I was all right; I was used to silly-placed video equipment and ducked!) I observed the load comprised three schoolgirls, obviously by this stage of the proceedings resigned to the fact that they wouldn't be in school on time and not unduly worried. The other people waiting at the stop all enquired where the bus was going, but none was tempted to board, and away we went.

Now in case it be thought I may be knocking the service, let it be said that the driver was immaculately attired, polite and friendly with an uncanny knack, it transpired, of totally disarming cold, wet passengers faced with getting to work late, by his pleasant and friendly demeanour. That at least was impressive. As for the coach, I was just glad I was only going as far as Heathrow and not to one of the far-flung destinations proclaimed on the side windows. I didn't have my tape measure with me, but if the seat spacing was legal, it was only just so!

Comings and goings of passengers were few and far between, although there were lots of enquiries from bedraggled people along the route as to where the bus might be going. Where passengers were picked up, boarding was dreadfully slow; on average single passengers took about a minute to board whilst two at a certain stop took about 90sec. It is probably just as well that there were never more than that.

Thandi had obviously done a good job with route-learning; the 555 is a convoluted route, but only once did the driver have to confirm a direction with his passengers, and little more time was lost, despite a delay to get through the cargo tunnel into Heathrow Central, and we arrived at Heathrow at 09.21, about 40 minutes down.

Now either the 556 at 09.20 had been the only Thandi coach of the morning to run to time (odd though that we never saw it as we approached Heathrow Central) or it never came, and instead I had to settle for the next 555 back to Shepperton, which turned up 18 minutes late with a dreadfully scruffy beige-coloured Duple-bodied Volvo B58 of indeterminate vintage in the livery of Astons of Worcester, not an operator one might be looking for on a service from Heathrow to Chertsey. Although the driver was less smartly attired than the earlier one, he was just as polite and friendly, and an

Left:
Thandi's Volvo B58 arrives late in Shepperton on the morning of 27 October. It is operating on the 555 from Chertsey to Heathrow.
Stephen Morris

uneventful journey ensued, though for much of the time I had the bus to myself, apart from an observer (incognito) from Surrey County Council who was out to have a look at things for himself.

So instead of going to Walton to pick up the 567, I alighted in Shepperton. Having looked at the timetable, which included no map, there was only one way the 567 could possibly pass through Shepperton to Staines, so I waited at the appropriate point. Two or three minutes after it was due, I happened to look the other way and, incredibly, there was the 567 with Staines on the front, coming in totally the opposite direction! It must still have been heading for Walton, with the wrong blind up, I thought, but no, at the end of the road where it would have had to turn right to cross Walton bridge, it turned left instead. Obviously this roundabout route was more roundabout than I had given it credit for! As the 567 runs only three times a day, I had to cheat. I dashed home, picked up the car and drove into Staines, where I managed to catch up with it before it left on its next journey to Walton, and yes, it did follow a much more roundabout route than I had believed possible. It covers at least two roads which have had no service that I can remember, though older-established residents of the area do recall them having been served a long time ago. This time the load was reasonable for at least the first half of the journey, but for the second half I was the sole passenger as the bus weaved around housing estates where residents couldn't *possibly* manage without a bus, but seemed to be managing all right that day. This time our London Country South West driver did get lost, emitting a loud expletive when he realised his mistake, but as he had left Staines on time and driven the Leyland National in a style which might euphemistically be described as flamboyant, he had several minutes in hand, and the bus rattled and banged in protest as it described a circle around a roundabout at an amazing rate of knots and shot off back to rejoin the route. We were still a good five minutes early into Walton, despite our added mystery tour.

In Walton I observed my first Thandi coach with a destination display. A Leopard this time. It proclaimed its destination as Birmingham.

And so, to round off the morning's ramblings, a green Leyland National on the 218 to Staines. Timing in Walton was spot on, to the minute, and the driver had no difficulty finding his way. But again, whether it was something to do with the competitive spirit I know not; it was loud pedal hard down all the way so that by Laleham we were well over five minutes early, which rather confused the natives, and even earlier into Staines.

So that was my first taste of deregulation. Not as exciting as some, but we still had a level of service almost the same as that before D-day. We had gained some reliability, it seemed, on the 218, but lost some on the Heathrow route, and it was soon apparent that Thandi's poor start had lost it some custom, probably for good. By the end of the day the rain had eased and my feet, physically-speaking, had thawed; but I think, mentally, they're still on the chilly side! And let it be said that a fortnight later I saw a Thandi coach — an Irish-registered Duple-bodied Volvo in a nondescript beige livery — on time and sporting a correct destination!

Below:
Fooled! A London Country B-series National heads out of Shepperton for Staines in the opposite direction to that which was expected on its first journey on 27 October.
Stephen Morris

Ian Cowley

Variety at Ipswich

Ian Cowley takes a look at his local bus operator, Ipswich Borough Transport — or Ipswich Buses as it became in 1986 — and demonstrates that there are photographic locations in the town other than Electric House and the adjacent bus station.

Above right:
Typifying the 51 Leyland Atlanteans in the Ipswich fleet is this Roe-bodied AN68 climbing out of the town up Bishops Hill in July 1986. It is named *Northdown*, after one of the Thames sailing barges which were once a common sight on the Suffolk coast. An Eastern Counties Leyland Leopard follows in the background.

Right:
From 1950 (when motorbus operation started) until 1968 Ipswich standardised on AECs. During that time it bought 60 Regents and this 1966 Regent V with Neepsend bodywork is seen in Cliff Lane on 2 August 1986 carrying a headboard to mark the last day of AEC Regent operation.

Left:
Operation of AEC single-deckers also ceased in 1986 with the withdrawal of the last of the Swifts. This was one of five with East Lancs bodywork. The bridge with the 12ft 3in headroom, marked by the warning sign on the left of the picture, dictates the use of single-deckers on routes to the Chantry Estate.

Right:
Second-hand vehicles have played but a small part in Ipswich's operations. Five ECW-bodied Bristol REs were purchased from Leicester City Transport in 1980 and when the last of the Regents were withdrawn this one became the oldest bus in regular service. It is seen at St Matthew's roundabout in the morning rush hour.

Left:
The Dennis Falcon is the standard Ipswich single-decker with 14 in operation. This 1986 bus has a unique style of East Lancs two-door bodywork; earlier deliveries were of a more angular appearance.

Top:
The newest Falcons have dual-door Northern Counties bodies as illustrated by this example in Princes Street, Edinburgh. The Falcons are named after birds of prey — this one is called *Peregrine*.

Left:
Although the Dennis Falcon is the Ipswich standard single-decker, Leyland have supplied four B21s. These were a frustrated export order and are the only examples of the type in operation in Britain. They were bodied by Alexander (Belfast) who also bodied a small batch of B21s for operation in Northern Ireland. This one is seen outside the Customs House.

Above:
Minibus operation commenced in September 1986 with this Northern Counties-bodied Dodge. Five Dodges are in use with a mixture of Northern Counties and East Lancs bodywork and the services are marketed under the Imp brand name. An East Lancs-bodied Atlantean and a Bristol RE follow.

Gavin Booth

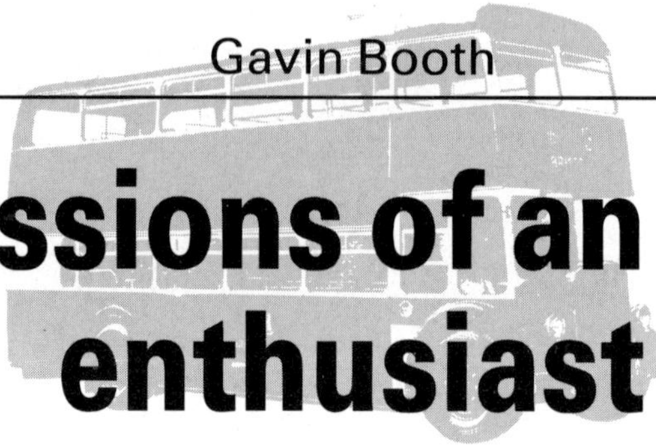

Confessions of an ageing enthusiast

In which retired *Annual* editor Gavin Booth reveals much about his enthusiasm and little about his age.

A long time ago in a galaxy far away — or so it seems — the bus enthusiast's lot was a happy one. Buses were orderly: soberly painted, normally red or green; big double-deckers with conductors; running predictably on properly licensed services.

The buses themselves were made in Britain, and said on the side in big letters where they came from — place-names you could recognise, like Aberdare, or Middlesbrough, or Swindon: none of your 'Cynon Valley', 'Cleveland' or 'Thamesdown' back in the 1950s. But what did it matter? The General Manager was in his office, and all was right with the world.

Coaches were slow and solid. Slow because they were not allowed to go faster than 40mph, and anyway there were no motorways to allow them to do much more. Solid because coach designers equated luxury with heavy moquettes, polished wood and bags of chrome. But if coaches were ponderous and expensive, no matter. There were railway services available as an option, and most coach operators had a comfortable cushion of profitable bus services to underwrite their express operation.

And what about the enthusiasts? Well, the first authenticated sighting of the species *griceris omniborum* was in 1929 when The Omnibus Society was formed. There are persistent rumours that the PSV Circle has been organising tours from Colchester since horse bus days, but perhaps it just seems like that.

Certainly enthusiasts were few and far between in the 1950s, as I recounted in an article in *Buses Annual 1974*, so you could safely visit a strange town without being ambushed by pen-carrying, camera-toting gricers. But gradually it became clear that you were not alone. Instead of furtively noting numbers and snatching snapshots, it was possible to come out of the closet and talk to like-minded souls who actually understood your enthusiasm.

Our point of contact was often *Buses Illustrated*, the quarterly predecessor of today's *Buses* and the magazine whose very existence reassured us that there was intelligent life on earth, if only in January, April, July and

Below:
'. . . place names you could recognise . . .' — Wallasey Corporation Motors Titans illustrate the point. *Harry Hay*

Do you give the Bus-spotters salute? ★

Ian Allan BUS-SPOTTERS CLUB

★ Ian Allan Bus-spotters Club members greet one another with the " bus-stop sign "—raise your left hand to the left, elbow bent and palm of hand facing forward, as if you are hailing a bus. This is the private greeting of one Ian Allan Bus-spotter to another, and just one of the ways in which you can meet new friends when you join this Club with nation-wide membership.

● TO JOIN, all you have to do is to fill in the form overleaf, cut out this page and send it with the necessary remittance to :

Ian Allan BUS-SPOTTERS CLUB (BSE),
Craven House,
Hampton Court,
East Molesey, Surrey.

Ian Allan Publications About Road Transport

Bus ABC's

ABC LONDON TRANSPORT Trams and Trolleybuses	2/-
ABC BIRMINGHAM CITY Trams and Trolleybuses	2/6
ABC BIRMINGHAM CITY Buses ...	2/6
ABC BRISTOL Buses and Coaches ...	2/6
ABC MIDLAND RED Buses and Coaches	2/-
ABC RIBBLE Buses and Coaches ...	2/-

★ ★ ★

LONDON'S DOUBLE-DECKER BUSES	2/6

In preparation :

OVERGROUND By S. A. Newman (2nd Edition) ...	2/6

Other Road Transport ABC's

ABC BRITISH ROAD SERVICES ...	2/-
ABC BRITISH CARS (new edition) ...	2/-
ABC AMERICAN CARS	2/-

In preparation :

ABC MOTORCYCLES	2/-

From all Bookstalls and Booksellers

277/132/150/1052 *Printed in Great Britain in the City of St. Albans by Gibbs & Bamforth Ltd.*

October. Alan Townsin, editor of *BI*, was the fount of all human knowledge. For *BI* we had to thank Ian Allan, who saw an opportunity to diversify from railways. Many of us started as Locospotters, and moved on to buses.

It was less easy to be a *real* spotter, though. OK, there was the Ian Allan Bus Spotters Club, but I didn't join it, and I have met very few people who will admit they did. But there were not the *ABCs*. Unless you lived in London, or Birmingham, or Bristol, or the Midlands, or East Kent, you had no numbers to underline. We bought the handful of bus *ABCs* and read them over and over again. There was nothing else to read, so we became experts in distinguishing a London 3RT3 from a 3RT3/1, or a Midland Red S6 from an S8. But if you never got to London or the Midlands, that was not a lot of use.

New bus books were rare. The 1950s equivalent of today's close-set page listing bus books from a dozen publishers, on the inside cover of *Buses*, would have been a three-line small ad. A new bus book was an event — although it was usually a book about London. We bought the books, of course, in the absence of anything else, and we knew the history of London General and London Transport inside out. The things I could tell you about Frank Pick . . .

We took photographs with the best cameras we could afford — Box Brownies, Brownie 127s, then maybe the Ilford Sportsman or the Kodak Retinette. Today the combined value of cameras, lenses and tripods on the average enthusiasts' trip would pay my mortgage for several years.

In the 1950s, enthusiasts' trips were exciting and unpredictable. Our intelligence network was unsophisticated, so we were regularly genuinely surprised by what we saw. Bus rallies and company open days had not been invented, so the summer weekends were free for exploration. Apart from London Transport, again, preserved buses did not really exist — or rather they did exist, but they were still running in service.

Then suddenly all of that changed. But what changed — the world or me? Probably a bit of both. The Change came with changing interests. I know of friends — no names, no pack-drill — who grice to their heart's content until the day that Love taps them gently on the shoulder. The Change is spectacular. Instead of a camera, a young lady is worn on the arm, and conversation is steered firmly away from buses

Above:
'... enthusiasts' trips were exciting ...' — this group at Halifax on the eve of the creation of the West Yorkshire PTE look suitably excited by the impending change.
Stewart J. Brown Collection

on to three-piece suites, double-glazing and rateable values. In all but a few cases the affliction is purely temporary, and once the first flush of Love wears off, there is a gradual return to normality. Before you dismiss me as a misogynist, let me assure you that I write from experience. Looking back at the valiant efforts I made to avoid chasing, photographing or even acknowledging buses in some fascinating places, in my efforts not to discourage the girl of the moment, I cannot help feeling that a box of slides would in some ways be a more meaningful memento than a few poignant memories. Ho hum.

There is the reverse to this, of course. The enthusiast who forsakes women for buses. Having met some, this may be just as well. Inevitably, though, your enthusiasms wane.

At one time I could quote from memory a string of trivia about the Edinburgh Corporation or Scottish Omnibuses fleets — registration numbers, seating capacities, month delivered, even the odd chassis number. But then I asked myself: 'why?' All the information I would ever want, and much more, was given in a flood of publications.

And so from a broad-brush interest, cultivated from the days when you read each issue of *Buses Illustrated* from cover to cover, several times over, your interest can become more specialised.

Bus enthusiasm has become such a wide-ranging hobby; from the days of simply underlining numbers, it has progressed to take in an ever-growing list of subcultures. Some I have studiously avoided, like bus modelling, tape-recording bus noises, or 138-depots-in-a-day 'Griceathons'. Equally there are others that have me in their grasp, like photography, driving buses, and actually travelling on them.

As you get older you find that bus enthusiasts, like policemen, seem to get younger. Certainly there are a lot of them, which is a healthy sign, who seem, not unnaturally, interested in the minutiae of Metrobuses and Nationals, with no interest in Really Fascinating Subjects like Edinburgh Corporation's tram-replacement Leylands, or the vehicle-buying policies of the BET Group. Some of them don't even know who Alan Townsin is!

I occasionally adopt the alter ego of Norman Griceworthy, particularly when asked to speak to gatherings of enthusiasts. Norman is an amalgam of the distinguishing features of all the enthusiasts you ever met — particularly the most eccentric. He wears a beret and a badge-bedecked anorak, and carries a bag that contains the basic essentials for indulging in the hobby, namely: a bottle of Tizer, a Mars bar (usually past its 'Sell By' date), a Woolworths notebook, more pens than anyone could ever use up in a lifetime, a multitude of dog-eared fleetlists, a copy of *The Bus Book* (only £4.95, buy it now), an Instamatic camera, a Kodachrome 35mm film (ie wrong size), a street map of Barnsley and a bus timetable (London Transport, circa 1978).

Norman is very keen. He knows much more about buses than anyone has the right, or the need, to know. And he will share his knowledge with everyone in earshot. His staying-power is legendary. No garage is missed, no bus station avoided, no scrapyard passed. An early start is no problem for the dedicated gricer, and what else is there to do in the evenings, anyway? We have all met Norman Griceworthy, or at least elements of his personality. We have probably all behaved the Griceworthy way.

Below:
'... I could quote from memory a string of trivia about the Scottish Omnibuses fleet ...' B807 (USC807) was an AEC Reliance, chassis number 2MU3RV2991, and it had an Alexander C41F body, number 6309. It entered service in June 1960. *Stewart J. Brown Collection*

It is hardly surprising, therefore, that some ageing enthusiasts choose not to wear their hobby on their sleeves. We avoid the more obvious embellishments like the lapel-badges, the ever-ready notebook, the pocketful of pens, the haversack, the Tizer bottle. The main giveaway is probably the camera-case. At a pinch we *could* be landscape or wildlife photographers (the acceptable face of camera-carrying), except, perhaps, in Airdrie or Walsall on a November day, when our cover is blown.

As age creeps on, the comforts become more important. The car rather than the bike or the feet (or even the bus, I fear, on occasions); the warm pub rather than the Mars bar and Tizer on a windswept bus station; and the prospect of avoiding rabid dogs in a Barnsley scrapyard never appealed, even when I could run that fast.

The Woolworths notebook has been replaced by discreet notes in my leather-bound diary, and then only about developments in Edinburgh. Judging from the flow of information reaching Gordon Watts for *Buses*, and the output of the PSV Circle and the various fleetlist publishers, there are plenty of notebooks in action on Britain's streets already, and doubtless a few well-loaded home computers too. That

is the theory. In fact, we probably never shake off the most basic facets of our hobby. Scratch the surface of the most distinguished-looking middle-aged enthusiast and you will find Norman Griceworthy lurking somewhere underneath.

In many ways it is rewarding to see how much the hobby has grown, for this helps guarantee a positive attitude on the part of bus operators, manufacturers and publishers, the people we all need to keep our interest going. It is good to see how many enthusiasts find their way into the bus industry, for in times of stress, a bit of positive interest can go a long way. So — are things better than they were 30 years ago? Probably. Does today's enthusiast have it too easy? Probably. Has all the interest gone from the hobby? I hope not.

So, however good my intentions, I still find myself on street corners, furtively photographing buses. Patience, which my wife will testify is never normally one of my virtues, is

Top:
Norman Griceworthy collecting bus numbers . . . *John Burnett*

Left:
. . . and recording bus sounds. ('I wonder why these modern buses are all so quiet?') *John Burnett*

still paramount when an interesting bus is promised. And I still stand in line with 50 assorted enthusiasts to photograph a new livery on a depot visit, experiencing that rare sensation as 51 focal-plane shutters simultaneously click, and 51 identical photos are made for posterity. So maybe we don't ever grow up — and maybe that's no bad thing.

And a footnote. There are grown men, some even older than I am, whose Christmas Day is only complete when their stocking contains the latest copy of *Buses Annual*. Men who wear dark suits. Men who are respected pillars of the community. Educated men. Cultured men. Men who spend five difficult months resisting all temptation to peek into the *Annual* in bookshops, so that they can savour that moment on Christmas morning as eagerly as a five-year old with a new bike.

A Happy Christmas to all of you.

Right:
'... discreet notes in my leather-bound diary ...' — Gavin Booth formally illustrating the respectable (?) face of bus enthusiasm. *John Burnett*

Below:
'... experiencing that rare sensation as 51 focal-plane shutters simultaneously click ...' *Stewart J. Brown*

Roy Marshall

Looking back

Roy Marshall, whose name is well known to many enthusiasts and whose first published bus picture appeared on the cover of *Buses Illustrated* in 1950, looks back over his 40 years as an enthusiast employed in the bus business.

My first job on leaving school at Easter in 1946 was with Skill's of Nottingham, where I secured a clerical post at a time when jobs in public transport were hard to find because of ex-servicemen returning to their former employers. Skill's ran a mixture of stage, works, contract, private hire, express and excursion operations and had a 40-strong fleet made up of Bedford, Dennis, Guy, Leyland and TSM chassis. Their livery — inspired by a carnation buttonhole — was two shades of green, with pink on coaches.

Three Daimler CVD6s with metal-framed Duple bodies were scheduled for delivery in 1950. However a drop in private hire business,

Plate 1

Plate 2

caused by a combination of increased car ownership and a resurgence of activity by British Railways forced a reduction in capital expenditure and two of the Daimlers were sold to Gash of Newark before being delivered.

The third, shown at East Bridgford terminus in August 1950 (**Plate 1**), incorporated my ideas in some of the details — the interior trim, the livery, and the twin destination indicators. The last-named was a feature which I was to specify in all of those undertakings in which I had a say on such matters. This Daimler ran for Skill's until 1954.

Skill's were among the early operators of underfloor-engined coaches with both a Leyland Royal Tiger and an AEC Regal IV. There were to have been two AECs, but only one was built and it had 43-seat Harrington bodywork. I wanted it to have a straight waistline and roofline so that the body would not date too quickly. Half-drop windows with glass louvres were specified to provide the best ventilation in all weathers. This bus (**Plate 2**) was new in 1951 and is seen loading for the Newton air display in 1954 — by which time I had moved to Nottingham City Transport.

I joined NCT as a traffic clerk in 1951. The oldest batch of buses still intact at this time comprised 46 AEC Regents with 7.7-litre engines and preselector gearboxes which had been delivered in 1938-39. They had Metro-Cammell steel-framed bodies with single-skin roofs and no interior lining panels and this gave a creditable unladen weight of under seven tons for a 54-seat bus. An example (**Plate 3**) is seen in the city centre in the summer of 1953.

When I joined NCT it had a fleet of some 250 motorbuses and 150 trolleybuses and it was the latter which had attracted me to the undertaking. Shortly after I started, the last of 102 BUT 9641T three-axle 70-seaters were delivered. These had Brush bodies — although I preferred the smaller, and livelier, four-wheelers which had been delivered earlier.

Plate 3

Plate 4

Plate 5

Plate 6

An evocative picture taken in January 1953 (**Plate 4**) includes five buses and not a single car. One of the three inspectors on the right — the man in the centre — was the mechanical inspector with his bag of tools to rectify minor faults. The motorbus on the left was one of 45 Craven-bodied Regents delivered in 1937 whose bodies gave endless trouble; the extra cost of a Metro-Cammell body would, with hindsight, have been money well spent. Loudspeakers to make traffic announcements are visible on poles on the right of the picture.

After seven years in Nottingham I moved in September 1958 to Southport Corporation where I was traffic superintendent. The smart fleet of almost 80 vehicles was painted red and cream and included 16 open-top buses used only in the summer. Four of these were elderly Leyland Titan TD3 double-deckers with English Electric bodies; the remainder were ex-army Bedford QLs some of which had four-wheel drive and were operated on the sands.

It was in one of these Titans that I passed my PSV driving test after mastering the change from third to top gear (wait and dip the clutch lightly). In 1962 the TD3s were effectively replaced by postwar PD2s but they were retained for carrying passengers along the shore between Ainsdale and Southport Pier because they could carry over twice as many people as the 23-seat Bedford QLs. No conductors were carried — the service did not use the public highway — but the shore did have patches of soft sand and on occasion a Titan would get bogged down, as happened in August 1963 (**Plate 5**).

There were a few wartime Daimlers and postwar Crossleys and AEC Regent IIIs in the fleet but Southport was basically a Leyland user, standardising on the PD2 which gave exemplary service. When Leyland ceased building bodies, Weymann bodywork was specified and a 1964 view in the town centre (**Plate 6**) shows a Weymann-bodied PD2/20 (one of 16) alongside a 1947 all-Leyland product. Bright livery layouts like this became popular in the late 1960s — almost 20 years after its adoption by Southport.

In July 1966 I was appointed Omnibus Manager of Gelligaer Urban District Council. There were 30 buses in the fleet: three Titan

Plate 7

PD2s, nine Regal IIIs, four Tiger PS1s, and 14 AEC Reliances. The red, green and grey livery was a wartime adaptation of the prewar red, green and white which had been based on the colours of the Welsh flag. I reintroduced the prewar colours on two former demonstrators — an AEC Swift and a Leyland Panther, both with 53-seat Willowbrook bodies. These had been bought to replace 35-seat half-cab single-deckers — such as the Regal which is about to pass the Panther (**Plate 7**) — whose capacity was inadequate for the undertaking's extensive school operations. The selective purchase of second-hand buses such as these ex-demonstrators to minimise capital expenditure was a policy I employed in each of the undertakings which I managed.

Three (out of a maximum of four) double-deckers were still operated and it had been planned that they would be replaced by 45-seat underfloor-engined single-deckers. The double-deck route from Rhymney bridge to Bargoed and Ystrad Mynach was co-ordinated with services of Red & White, Western Welsh and the Bedwas & Machen UDC to form an extended route via Caerphilly to Newport. For this three Bristol VRTs with Northern Counties bodies were ordered, the Bristol being chosen as it was the only model which appeared to offer a specification suitable for 40mph operation while still being capable of climbing the steep hills in Bargoed and Newport. The schedules called for each vehicle to operate 2,000 miles on a six-day week. **Plate 8** shows one of the VRs passing through Caerphilly on its way to Newport.

My next move was to Burton-upon-Trent, where I became General Manager in February 1971. The fleet at that time comprised 13 Guy Arabs, 24 Daimler CSG5s and CCG5s and six Daimler Fleetlines. The livery was madder and cream. Apart from the Fleetlines, all of Burton's buses had five-cylinder Gardner engines and most had 12-volt electrics. This combination made for starting difficulties, but certainly gave commendable fuel consumption.

Most of the bodywork was by Massey Brothers of Wigan, as shown on the smart Daimler photographed in October 1971 (**Plate 9**). The bodies were trouble-free . . . which is more than can be said for the David Brown gearboxes on the CSG5s.

I introduced one-man operation to Burton, using three single-deck Fleetlines which had been delivered prior to my arrival and augmented by four ex-Bournemouth single-deckers. **Plate 10** shows one of a pair of Park Royal-bodied Tiger Cubs which I had painted in Gelligaer-style red, white and green. The

Plate 8

NEWPORT
Caerphilly 150

e 9

2 HARPER AVENUE VIA STATION
Naturally..
REDIFFUSION COLOUR TV
MARSHALLS
TFA 987

Plate 10 Civic Society in Burton had complained that the town's buses were too drab and while my attempt to introduce the former East Midland livery of biscuit, cream and chocolate was unsuccessful, the Transport Committee did accept the Gelligaer livery and this was adopted from 1972.

In June 1974 I moved to what was to be my longest appointment as General Manager of the newly-formed Burnley & Pendle Joint Transport Committee which on 1 April of that year had succeeded the 41-year-old Burnley, Colne & Nelson operation. The fleet here totalled 128 buses in what approximated to the original Burnley Corporation madder and cream livery with red (in place of orange) beading. This was modified by increasing the amount of cream to display a black and red Burnley & Pendle fleetname and later a deeper shade of cream was introduced to eliminate fading. On coaches the lighter cream was retained and used with biscuit and chocolate: after 20 years East Midland's original livery had at last reappeared! The black and red fleetname — inspired by the use of similar colours by Southern Electricity — was another feature I adopted at each of the fleets which I managed.

BCN had been a pioneer in introducing one-man operation of single-deckers in the 1950s and the fleet was mainly single-decked — Tiger Cubs, Panthers, Bristol REs, Seddon RUs and Leyland Nationals. One all-day service was still double-decked, using Leyland Titan PD2As with forward-entrance bodies.

One batch of Bristol REs had Seddon bodywork. The order had originally been placed with East Lancs but was transferred to Seddon after a fire at the East Lancs factory interrupted production. The front-end was poorly supported and the bodies had to be rebuilt; **Plate 11** shows a rebuilt example in a typical Burnley setting — terraced houses, a mill chimney and Pendle Hill.

Leyland Leopards with East Lancs bodies were bought for routes extended in to Pendleside villages. The first had flat fronts and the airflow caused problems with a build up of dirt on the driving mirrors. So the second batch had curved corners and BET-style windscreens as seen in **Plate 12** on an example leaving Reedley Hallows in 1980 when it was new.

Burnley & Pendle was not only my longest appointment, it was also my last and after 40 years of enthusiasm in the bus business I opted for early retirement in 1986 — to allow still more time for enthusiasm as an onlooker, as well as expansion of my other interests and responsibilities — not the least being my family!

Plate 11

Plate 12

Ian Train

Routemasters in Scotland

Before 1985 the idea of Routemasters in Scotland was inconceivable. But now it is an established fact. Ian Train provides photographic proof.

Below:
The first Routemaster to run for the Scottish Bus Group was RM652 which was borrowed by Clydeside in the summer of 1985. It is seen here in full London livery — but with Scottish advertising — on Clydeside's service from Paisley to Glasgow via Thornliebank.

Left:
Clydeside quickly decided that it had a role for the Routemaster and 46 were purchased during 1985-86. They are normally used on local services in or near Glasgow; RM416 made the 30-mile trip to Ayr, where it is seen here, to coincide with an open day at Western's Kilmarnock depot.

Below:
Sister Glasgow-area company Kelvin borrowed two of Clydeside's Routemasters and decided to buy some of its own — 59 in all. These entered service in the summer of 1986 and RM408 is seen in Glasgow's Argyle Street on a new five-minute frequency service introduced to compete with Strathclyde PTE.

Above:
The other SBG company to buy Routemasters was Strathtay, whose RM42 is seen here on loan to Eastern operating a shuttle service between Edinburgh and Dalkeith to serve the August 1986 Lothian Country Fair. Strathtay have 20 Routemasters.

Left:
Stagecoach, the Perthshire independent, was the first operator of Routemasters in Scotland. RM1599 is seen in the former McLennan garage at Spittalfield while being prepared for service. Stagecoach acquired the old-established McLennan business in 1985.

Above:
Routemaster variety is provided by this one-time Northern General bus, acquired by Stagecoach from Stevenson of Uttoxeter. It is seen loading in Perth on a service operated jointly with Strathtay. It has a Leyland engine, which justifies the fitting of a Leyland badge on the heater intake grille above the cab.

Right:
London's FRM1 made a brief sortie to Scotland in 1986 on what must have been one of its longest-ever trips. It attended an open day at Clydeside's Greenock depot . . . in what any Scot will recognise as typical Greenock weather.

Above:
Three Routemasters are seen here at the SBG Engineering workshops at Kilmarnock in July 1986. Their previous identities are RM678 (WLT 678), 774 (WLT 774) and 983 (WLT 983), all are in 'LB' red and await partial overhaul and repainting. *Maxwell H. Fowler*

Left:
Routemaster 293 (VLT 293) undergoing partial overhaul and repainting at Kilmarnock. Photographed during a works open day in August 1986; this bus is now with Kelvin Scottish, as are the vehicles in the above photo.
Maxwell H. Fowler

Right:
The modern livery used by Kelvin Scottish sits slightly uneasily on the traditional shape of the Routemaster. This one is seen in central Glasgow on the frequent service to Easterhouse.
Stewart J. Brown

Kelvin SCOTTISH
5
Clydebank Partick
Argyle St. Duke St.
Carntyne Edinburgh Rd.
EASTERHOUSE
Kelvin SCOTTISH
RM774
WLT 774

Stewart J. Brown

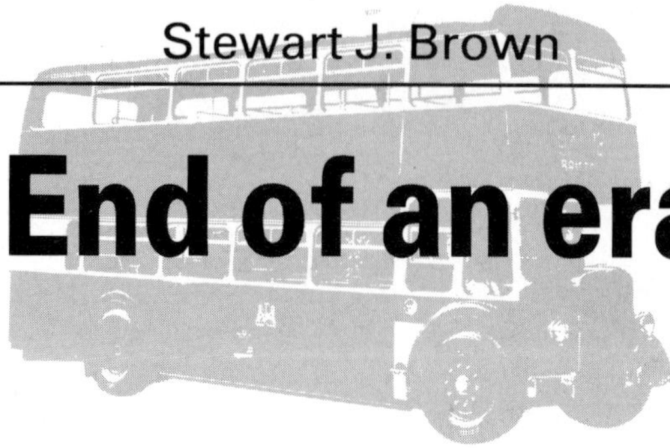

End of an era

Bedford buses and coaches were once inseparable from independent operation. Now Bedfords are no more. Stewart J. Brown traces the history of one of Britain's most popular marques.

In the late 1970s one in every three coaches was a Bedford, that marque beloved by independent operators for the best part of 50 years. Bedford consistently outsold not only arch-rivals Ford but also the combined forces of AEC and Leyland. Then in 1980 as imported coaches began to appear in quantity Bedford sales dropped from a peak of almost 1,000 a year to a low of around 200 in 1983. And there they stayed. A victim of changing tastes, Bedford launched the Venturer to give more power and a better ride . . . but it was too late in coming. At the end of 1986 the unthinkable happened. Bedford ceased building coach chassis.

Bedfords were always comparatively simple low-cost chassis, designed very much for the small operator who often had rudimentary maintenance facilities. By using parts produced for high-volume trucks, Bedford kept down the cost of their bus and coach chassis and sold them at prices well below those charged by the builders of heavyweights. And, of course, once a body was fitted to a mid-engined Y-series Bedford the end product was virtually indistinguishable — except to those of us in the know — from much more expensive chassis. Many operators adopted the fairly reasonable logic that the passengers only noticed the body anyway and that it was therefore preferable to buy a Bedford and update the fleet more often, than to buy a heavyweight which would have to be kept longer to repay the extra capital invested in it. In a fashion-conscious business a modern coach was an asset.

The Bedford name appeared in April 1931 on a 2-ton truck chassis produced at the Luton

Below:
A trio of Bedfords which summarises the development of the marque. On the right a 1931 WHB, in the centre a standard postwar OB with typical Duple Vista bodywork, and on the left a 1973 YRQ with Duple Dominant body, newly delivered to Theobald's Coaches of Long Melford. Note the matching registrations of the OB and the YRQ.
Bedford

Right:
Carrying appropriate registration letters an early SB with Duple body in the ownership of West Coast Motors of Campbeltown. SBs of this type, where the bodywork incorporates Bedford's front cowl, were usually petrol-engined.
Stewart J. Brown

Below right:
By 1965, when this SB was delivered to Central of Walsall, virtually all new Bedford psvs were diesel-powered. This one has Duple Bella Vega bodywork.
Stewart J. Brown

factory of Vauxhall Motors, since 1925 a subsidiary of the US General Motors organisation. Vauxhall had previously been building small Chevrolet trucks; these were soon replaced by the expanding range of new Bedford models. The first PSV chassis — the WHB and WLB — appeared before the end of 1931 and set the pattern for Bedford buses and coaches for the next 20 years. They were of normal control layout with the driver sitting behind the engine and front axle. The engine was a 44bhp 3.2-litre six-cylinder petrol unit. The WHB was designed for 14-seat bodywork while the longer-wheelbase WLB was nominally a 20-seater. Bedford claimed a 52% share of the market for 14-20 seat buses in the last quarter of 1931 which is perhaps more indicative of the skill of the company's public relations men in manipulating statistics than of Bedford's real impact on the bus business.

Be that as it may, the small Bedfords were undeniably a success and the competition in this segment of the market was soon overwhelmed as Bedfords found their way into both large and small fleets which had a need for small buses or coaches. The WHB was discontinued in 1933 and the WLB was succeeded by the WTB in 1935, although some WTL goods chassis were fitted with bus bodies for a period between the demise of the WLB and the appearance of the WTB. The WTB was a 3-ton chassis (the WLB had been a 2-ton model) and it could be fitted with 26-seat bodywork. It used a higher-powered version of the 3.2-litre petrol engine. The WTB was scheduled for replacement by the new OB in 1939, production of which had barely started when war broke out. Instead Bedford was authorised to build the only single-deck bus chassis to be available during the war — the OWB. This perpetuated the use of a petrol engine (since 1937 a 3.5-litre 72bhp unit) and some 3,300 OWBs were built between 1942 and 1945. Most were delivered to small operators.

The famous and ubiquitous OB reappeared in 1945 and was generally used as a 29-seat coach, more often than not with Duple's attractive Vista body. Arguably the most famous Bedford PSV, almost 13,000 were built when production ceased in 1950.

The OB's replacement was launched at the 1950 Commercial Motor Show. Along with its new S-series trucks Bedford announced the SB, the company's biggest bus yet — a 33-seater. The forward-control SB was still petrol-powered — now using a new 110bhp 4.9-litre engine (known as the 300, its capacity in cubic inches) — but a Perkins diesel option was available from 1953. The SB reflected Bedford's continued approach to gradual model development — bigger and heavier trucks, accompanied by similarly bigger and heavier bus and coach chassis. The SB was destined to be the British PSV chassis with the longest unbroken production run — 36 years.

Production of Bedford chassis was moved to a new factory in Dunstable in 1955, and at this time the wheelbase of the SB was extended to enable it to be fitted with maximum-length (30ft) bodywork able to carry up to 41 seated passengers. Early SBs were delivered with a bulbous front scuttle which some coachbuilders incorporated in their bodywork; on later versions this feature could be deleted, allowing

Above:
For operators requiring a bus smaller than the OB, Bedford offered the OLAZ truck chassis, which looked generally similar but was smaller. This one had a Duple body and was new in 1952 to MacBrayne of Glasgow. It is seen here in service with Invercarron of Stonehaven in 1966. *Stewart J. Brown*

Below:
The SB was the coach on which many independent operators built their businesses. This one was in the eight-vehicle fleet of Moody's Coaches of Northfleet when photographed outside Victoria Coach Station in 1973.
Stewart J. Brown

Above:
Bedford's smaller models were ideal for touring in out-of-the-way places. Alexander (Midland) used VAS coaches with Duple bodies on tours to the Scottish Highlands. Ths one is seen on the Kyle of Lochalsh ferry.
Stewart J. Brown

Below:
Comparatively few Bedfords were to be found in NBC fleets. This VAM70 was actually a pre-NBC purchase, having been bought by Wilts & Dorset in 1968. It had a 40-seat Willowbrook body, unusual in being of two-door layout. *Stewart J. Brown*

Left:
A contrast in VALs. Most were coaches, as illustrated by this Plaxton-bodied vehicle participating in the 1965 Blackpool Coach Rally — when 28 out of 47 entries were Bedfords. Less common were VAL buses. This one, with Duple (Midland) bus bodywork, was also new in 1965 and is seen here soon after entering service with Irvine of Salsburgh.
Bedford, Stewart J. Brown

coachbuilders to construct front ends to their own designs. The first Bedford diesel engine, based on the petrol 300, was produced in 1957 and appeared as an option in the SB; the Perkins diesel engine was then dropped from Bedford PSVs.

The VAS, the spiritual successor to the OB, was launched in 1961 with a choice of petrol or diesel engines. The former was a 100bhp 3.52-litre (214cu in) unit; the latter was the 97bhp 4.93-litre engine previously used in the SB, which now had a 5.42-litre (330cu in) 105bhp engine. The VAS was designed to be the basis of a 29-seat coach, reintroducing a purpose-built PSV chassis of this size after a gap of 10 years during which a small number of O and C-series truck chassis had been modified to accept bus or coach bodies where operators required a smaller vehicle than the SB.

The VAS was followed by the most striking Bedford of them all, the twin-steer VAL, in 1962. By adopting this layout Bedford were able to produce a 36ft-long coach chassis without using new heavy-duty components. The twin front axles were able to cope with the weight of the engine in the front overhang and by using 16in wheels (the same as on the VAS) Bedford allowed bodybuilders to build comparatively low-floored vehicles. The standard power unit in the VAL was Leyland's 131bhp 6.54-litre O.400 engine. The 90bhp 5.76-litre Leyland O.350 was already available as an option in the SB but was soon replaced by the 115bhp O.370.

The V-range of PSVs was completed in 1965 with the launch of the VAM. This was a nominal 10m-long chassis with the engine in the front overhang and with a set-back front axle which allowed a front entrance. The VAM had the choice of Bedford's 330 diesel or 300 petrol engines, or the Leyland O.400 as used in the VAL. The range now comprised the 29-seat VAS, the 41-seat SB, the 45-seat VAM, and the 52-seat VAL.

In 1967 a 466cu in Bedford diesel engine

replaced the Leyland O.400 in the VAL and in the VAM, and the 330cu in diesel replaced the 300cu in unit in the VAS.

The next new model saw Bedford adopt the mid-engined layout for the first time with the 10m YRQ, launched in 1970. However, unlike most other mid-engined chassis which used horizontal engines, the YRQ was powered by a vertical engine to keep costs down by using components which were common to trucks. Bedford were able to install a vertical engine because of revisions to the regulations covering ground clearance. The engine was in fact the same 150bhp 466cu in unit used in the VAL and the VAM; the latter was replaced by the new YRQ, the former by the 11m long YRT, of similar layout to the YRQ but with a longer wheelbase, which appeared in 1972. The VAS and the SB continued in small-scale production.

The YRQ and YRT were superseded by the YLQ and YMT respectively in 1975. These had Bedford's new 8.2-litre 500 engine rated at 138bhp in the YLQ and 157bhp in the bigger YMT.

An interesting cul-de-sac in the Bedford bus story is the JJL which was announced at the 1976 Commercial Motor Show. This broke with Bedford tradition in having a rear-mounted engine, a vertical 330 diesel, which drove through an Allison AT540 automatic gearbox (Allison automatics were by this time an option on Y-series models) and a Morse Hi-Vo chain transfer box. The JJL was a low-floor midibus with integral (and stylish) bodywork by Marshall. A prototype was shown at the 1976 Show in London, and further prototypes were demonstrated to operators. However, the JJL was expensive (it was not much cheaper than a Leyland National) and in the late 1970s British bus operators had yet to discover small vehicles. Consequently the JJL never went into production.

In 1980 a revised version of the 500 engine, known as the Blue Series, was installed in the Y family of coach chassis. This was rated at 160bhp and the change was marked by the YLQ becoming the YMQ. A 206bhp turbocharged version of the 500 engine appeared in the Y-series in 1981 — this model was the YNT which at its launch had the highest power-to-weight ratio of any British production coach chassis. The original models had a Turner gearbox; this was replaced in 1981 by a ZF S6-65. To meet more stringent noise regulations the naturally-aspirated engines of the YMQ and YMT were replaced by derated versions of the turbocharged engine in 1982.

The VAS and the SB, or the PJK and NJM as they had been known since 1968 in GM computer-speak, had been updated in various ways throughout the years. The driving position had been improved in 1975; the braking system had been updated in 1978, and in 1982 the option of a turbocharged version of the 330 diesel engine was introduced.

Below:
The SB soldiered on to the end, although with few takers for psv operation. Aberconway bought a pair in 1976. They were SB5s with 41-seat Willowbrook bodies of a design which had altered little since the late 1950s.
Stewart J. Brown

Above:
Hants & Dorset also ran Bedford's three-axle VAL. This is a 1970 VAL70 with a 49-seat Duple body. It was originally a Wilts & Dorset coach. *Stewart J. Brown*

Below:
Simonds of Botesdale in Norfolk operated this Bedford Y-series with Duple Dominant bus body on stage carriage services. *Stewart J. Brown*

Above:
Rare Marshall Camair bodywork was fitted to this 1973 YRT in the Hedingham & District fleet. It was photographed in Colchester bus station soon after entering service. *Stewart J. Brown*

Below:
Maidstone Borough Transport standardised on Bedfords in the late 1970s and early 1980s. This Wadham Stringer-bodied YMT had automatic transmission and was one of five delivered in 1981. *Stewart J. Brown*

Interestingly the 300cu in petrol engine continued to be available in these vehicles, although few petrol-engined PSVs were specified for operation in Britain after the late 1950s. The model codes remained unchanged.

The YMQ became the YMP in 1984 to meet the requirements of the EEC's Vehicle Identification Number system (better known as the chassis number to the uninitiated) which prohibited the use of the letter Q. Shortened versions of the YMQ and the YMP, identified by an S suffix, were produced by Chassis Developments with Bedford's approval. A factory-built YMP-S was on the stocks when GM announced the cessation of coach chassis production.

In 1985 came the Venturer YNV, the first Bedford coach chassis to have a name. This was seen by industry observers as the chassis to recover Bedford's lost market share. Like all Bedfords before it, the Venturer was competitively priced. It was also 12m long; all previous Bedfords had been no more than 11m long (although some chassis had subsequently been lengthened by convertors). And it had air suspension, a feature which was *de rigueur* on a 1980s coach. With a gross vehicle weight of up to 16 tons, the Venturer was designed to carry the fashionable high-floor bodies being produced by most European coachbuilders. The YNV used the same engine and gearbox as the shorter YNT.

The Venturer was an attractively-specified chassis, and in 1986 Bedford sales started to creep up again. With deregulation and the privatisation of the National Bus Company it seemed fair to assume that there would be a growing demand for a cost-effective medium-weight chassis — not only for the top-of-the-range YNV for coach use, but also for the less-expensive YMQ and YMT which could form the basis of a low-priced bus where the operation was not so arduous as to need a high-cost heavyweight.

And then in September 1986 came the announcement. No more Bedford chassis. Bedford had been losing money and a plan to sell parts of Leyland Vehicles to General Motors had come to grief earlier in the year — in part at least because of incompetent handling of the matter by the Government, then Leyland's major shareholder. Had GM bought Leyland it is still probable that Bedford would have been closed. But perhaps some of the models would have survived in production in Lancashire. Now the Bedford marque name is no more, at least as far as bus and coach operators are concerned. The last home-market chassis was built at the end of 1986. Certain models continued in production as kits for overseas assembly, but it is difficult to see that lasting in the absence of a good home-market base on which to build.

Bedfords will remain a familiar sight on our roads for a few years to come. But by the end of this century they will have become rarities to be observed with great interest. A sad end for a 1970s market leader.

Left:
The Y-series models sold principally to independents but a few found their way into NBC fleets. This one was operated by National Travel (South East) and had Duple Dominant II bodywork. *Stewart J. Brown*

The Bedford Model Codes Pre-1968

Prior to the introduction of computer codings in 1968 most postwar models had their engine fitment identified by a suffix number or letter:

SBO	Perkins R6
SBG	Bedford 300cu in petrol
SB1	Bedford 300cu in diesel
SB3	Bedford 300cu in petrol
SB5	Bedford 330cu in diesel
SB8	Leyland O.350
SB13	Leyland O.370
VAS1	Bedford 300cu in diesel
VAS2	Bedford 214cu in petrol
VAS5	Bedford 330cu in diesel
VAL14	Leyland O.400
VAL70	Bedford 466cu in
VAM3	Bedford 300cu in petrol
VAM5	Bedford 330cu in diesel
VAM14	Leyland O.400
VAM70	Bedford 466cu in

Bedford Model Codes 1968 onwards

The computer codings used from 1968 showed the model line, the engine type, and the gross vehicle weight range. The main codes found on models for the UK market were:

Model line:

N	for the SB range
P	for the VAS range
T	for the VAM range
W	for the VAL
Y	for the mid-engined range

Engine:

J	330cu in diesel
L	500 derated
M	500 full power
N	500 turbocharged
R	466cu in diesel

GVW:

K	6.5 tons
M	9 tons
P	10 tons
Q	10 tons
T	12.5 tons
V	16 tons

Thus the YMT was a mid-engined chassis with the higher-powered 500 engine and a 12.5-ton GVW. The VAS and SB codes from the previous system were retained in Bedford publicity material until the end, although these models were also known as the PJK and NJM respectively.

Below:
A more typical combination — Bedford Y chassis, Plaxton body, and independent owner, in this case Globe of Barnsley. Alongside in this view on Blackpool promenade at the 1980 coach rally is a Bedford CF with Plaxton Mini-Supreme body, also owned by Globe.
Stewart J. Brown

The rear-engined JJL was an interesting diversion from Bedford's mainstream simple low-cost chassis. The JJL was bodied by Marshall of Cambridge to Bedford's designs but only prototypes were built. This one is seen in Brighton in 1985. *Stewart J. Brown*

Martin Curtis

Bristol's Lodekka

Bristol expert Martin Curtis traces the development of the once-ubiquitous Lodekka, one of the milestones of postwar bus chassis design.

From time to time in the motor industry there comes a model which transforms production of a particular class of vehicle by establishing new standards which rival manufacturers have then to match. Occasionally, the model's name may also take on a special significance in the process, being applied far more widely than simply to describe a specific model type. The BMC Mini is one example which readily springs to mind from the car building sector.

In the field of bus manufacturing several models have introduced revised layouts, including some which have been widely followed by other vehicle builders. However, among double-deck models few have created quite the sensation that Bristol achieved when it unveiled its Lodekka chassis. And whilst Bristol, sadly, is no longer with us as a bus manufacturer the legacy of its outstanding lowheight design may still be found in many modern double-deckers produced nearly 40 years after the original Lodekka prototype.

By the late 1940s two distinct types of double-decker bus had evolved. The 'highbridge' or normal height type was approximately 14ft 6in high and offered conventional

Below:
A 1957 LD6G in the Wilts & Dorset fleet typifies early Lodekkas. It is in the red livery used for Tilling fleets prior to the formation of NBC. *Stewart J. Brown*

Above:
The first Lodekka prototype of 1949, LDX001, was only 13ft 2in high when laden. It had a 58-seat ECW body which owed much to contemporary designs for the conventional Bristol K chassis. This bus operated for Bristol Tramways. *ECW*

forward-facing seating with central gangways on both decks. However, for routes which necessitated double-deckers in order to cope with heavy passenger loadings but on which there were height restrictions due to low bridges or other obstacles (with low

Table 1: Bristol Lodekka production totals

Chassis type	*Scottish Bus Group*	*Tilling Group*	*Total*
LDX	—	4	4
LD	578	1,601	2,179
LDL	—	6	6
LDS	—	8	8
FL	2	43	45
FSF	48	170	218
FS	100	790	890
FLF	376	1,491	1,867
Total Lodekkas	1,104	4,113	5,217

Right:
The second prototype, which ran for West Yorkshire, had bodywork with deeper windows. In both bodies there was an elongated bay over the rear wheels. *M. Fowler*

Right:
The 1,000th Lodekka was built in 1957 and went to Eastern National. It was handed over to Mr T. S. Gavin, Chairman of Eastern National (left) by Mr S. Kennedy, Chairman of the management board of the Tilling group.
BTC

railway bridges, in particular, being encountered rather more frequently than today) buses with 'lowbridge' bodywork — with an overall height of some 13ft 6in — were employed. The reduced height was achieved by fitting four-abreast seating and a sunken side gangway on the top deck. Unfortunately, such an arrangement was often unpopular with passengers and crews and much banging of heads followed owing to restricted headroom, not only upstairs but also on the lower deck below the sunken offside gangway. Consequently, not only was fare collection difficult on the top deck but passengers also found lowbridge buses to be awkward and very uncomfortable, especially when an inside passenger had to squeeze past as many as three other people to reach the top deck gangway. The lowbridge concept therefore involved a necessary yet most unsatisfactory interior layout.

In 1949 the Bristol Tramways & Carriage Co Motor Constructional Works, already much respected as a builder of very reliable passenger chassis, revealed a new design of double-decker bus which, overnight rendered the lowbridge layout obsolete. This was the semi-integral Lodekka (Low 'Decker) model which offered a conventional seating arrangement with central gangway on both decks, within the overall height of a lowbridge bus. To achieve this an extremely low-slung chassis was designed to which the lower deck floor and body frame were directly attached. This, in turn, allowed a significant reduction in the level of the lower deck floor, permitting a conventional top deck seating arrangement to be easily accommodated without exceeding an overall height of 13ft 6in.

Other features of the Bristol Lodekka chassis included a gearbox positioned immediately behind the forward-mounted engine, which resulted in a rearward facing seat (for five passengers) being fitted across the front bulkhead of the lower saloon which conveniently concealed this unit. The drive was then taken by a transmission shaft which was divided midway along the frame of the chassis to a separate final drive on each side of a revolutionary dropped-centre rear axle. Thus the customary layout of British double-deckers, with forward positioned engine and rear wheel drive, was retained.

Centrally down-swept chassis cross-members allowed the lower deck gangway to be depressed slightly below the remainder of the floor area. The gangway and floor levels were therefore extremely low, obviating the need for a step from the rear platform into the lower saloon. This caused some amusement when passengers, unfamiliar with this new type of bus, stepped heavily into the saloon where they expected the floor level to be raised! However, the ease with which entry could be made into the lower saloon soon came to be one of the most appreciated features of the Lodekka and established standards which few other buses of single or double-deck design have since matched. Indeed, even with the advent of urban minibuses, floor heights remain the source of complaints from many passengers who find steps within vehicles difficult to negotiate.

The first Lodekka prototype, registered LHY 949, was powered by a Bristol AVW 8¼-litre engine and displayed an exposed radiator of similar style to that seen on the Bristol M-types built the previous year. It was fitted with a 26ft long by 7ft 6in wide, 58-seat body, built, as in the case of all Bristol Lodekkas, by Eastern Coach Works of Lowestoft. The chassis number originally allocated was PT.149 but this was later changed to LDX.001. With fleet number C5000, this bus received a non-standard version of Bristol

Tramways' Tilling green and cream livery and was demonstrated to a number of other Tilling group operators before settling down to work on Bristol city services.

Unfortunately, having been nationalised as part of the Tilling group in 1948, neither Bristol nor ECW were able to supply their products to non-state owned concerns, much to the disappointment of many operators interested in the Lodekka who, for the time being at least, were compelled to persevere with traditional lowbridge vehicles.

In 1950, a second Lodekka prototype (chassis number LDX.002) appeared. Registered JWT 712, this bus became West Yorkshire 822 and was accordingly finished in a livery of Tilling red and cream. Whilst very similar in appearance to LHY 949, its ECW body included a number of detail differences, including deeper windows, but remained clearly derived from bodywork built by ECW for the conventional Bristol K series double-deck chassis. The chassis of LDX.002 also incorporated a number of modifications, the most significant being a revised drive layout with two full-length propeller shafts running along either side of the chassis which replaced the former, more complex design with the transmission split midway along the frame.

Extensive testing of both prototype Lodekkas followed — both with the operators in whose livery they were finished and with other state-owned bus companies — in a broad range of traffic conditions. Experience with these vehicles led, during 1953, to the construction of six preproduction LD type Lodekkas, one each being allocated to different Tilling operators including Bristol and West Yorkshire, together with Crosville, Hants & Dorset, United Counties and Western National respectively.

The benefit of lengthy trials with the prototypes resulted in several changes in design. Gone was the split transmission, replaced by a single propeller shaft running along the offside of the chassis to a redesigned dropped-centre rear axle. Also replaced was the wide exposed radiator and front bumper in favour of a more modern 'new-look front' with a long slotted grille. The bodywork had been considerably restyled without losing that unmistakable ECW look. The Lodekka's dimensions had also increased to 27ft long by 8ft wide to conform to the latest practice but retained seating for 58 passengers which, nevertheless, was more than normally accommodated in earlier lowbridge vehicles.

The six preproduction, Bristol-engined chassis were immediately followed by production Lodekkas from 1954 which were similar to the 1953 models but incorporated a number of small modifications, including a slatted grille and slightly lower bonnet.

An initial sanction of 200 LDs was built up to 1955, including 59 for Crosville Motor Services and 21 for Southern Vectis while most other Tilling fleets also received examples. From the same year, the first Scottish operators also took Lodekkas into stock when the Central SMT and Western SMT companies received 10 and 20 chassis respectively.

As production continued, further improvements in design followed, the most noticeable being the introduction of a much shorter and more attractive grille and, later, shorter front wings. During 1957, by which time Bristol's chassis-building business had been separated from the Bristol Tramways operating department to become Bristol Commercial Vehicles Ltd (though remaining under British Transport Commission control), six long-wheelbase LDL-type chassis were assembled with 70-seat ECW bodywork to the newly permitted 30ft maximum length. Two of these vehicles joined

Left:
The six trial LDL6Gs built in 1957 included this bus for Western National. The ECW body had a longer-than-normal bay behind the rear wheels. *ECW*

Right:
Before production of the flat-floor F-series Lodekkas commenced, eight LDS models were built and supplied to Brighton Hove & District. These were generally similar to the FS models which followed, although when new they had a blank front panel fitted with a winged Bristol motif. On vehicles which had the Cave-Browne-Cave heating system — identifiable by the cooling grilles flanking the destination box — the conventional radiator was dispensed with. *SJB*

Western National while the others were allocated to Bristol, Hants & Dorset, Notts & Derby and Thames Valley respectively.

Production of conventional Lodekkas, usually with 58 or 60 seat bodywork, had reached well over 1,500 vehicles by the late 1950s. Among major Tilling group customers with large LD fleets by this time were Bristol (143), Crosville (307), Eastern Counties (53), Eastern National (109), Hants & Dorset (77), Lincolnshire (59), Southern & Western National (84), Southern Vectis (60), United Counties (89), and West Yorkshire (73). In Scotland, the combined W. Alexander & Sons and Lawson fleets included 70 LDs while 71 were in service with Scottish Omnibuses, 69 with Central SMT and 101 with Western SMT.

In every case the engines used to power Lodekkas were either built by Bristol (including its later 8.9-litre BVW unit) or Gardner. Full LD production continued until 1959 although the Scottish group continued to

Below:
The bodywork on the FS-series Lodekka differed little from that fitted to the previous LD models. This is an FS6B with Bristol engine in the Southdown-BH&D fleet in 1973. It had been new in 1960 to Brighton Hove & District. The metal louvres over the side windows were a non-standard fitment. *Stewart J. Brown*

Left:
The prototype FSF was delivered to West Yorkshire. On production vehicles the sliding entrance door was abandoned by ECW in favour of double-jacknife doors. Forward entrance Lodekkas were fitted with bodywork which had a more upright front profile. *ECW*

receive examples until 1961, by which time over 2,100 chassis had been produced.

Two additional LDX prototypes were completed in 1958, though these were very different to those built in 1949-50. They became Crosville DLG949 (285 HFM) and Eastern National 1541 (236 LNO) and were classified type LDS (27ft long) and LDL (30ft long) respectively. Several advances distinguished these from earlier Lodekkas amongst which was the design of a completely flat floor, eliminating the slightly sunken lower deck gangway and the introduction of air suspension at the rear which allowed a constant height to be maintained regardless of load, while offering a superior quality of ride. The shorter version also featured revised window spacing and Cave-Browne-Cave heating and ventilating with heat exchangers fitted alongside the destination equipment, which resulted in the removal of a normal radiator and replacement of the traditional grille by a Bristol-ECW winged motif.

LDX.003 and 004 became the forerunners of a new generation of flat-floor F-series Lodekkas, built from 1959, but before the new range entered full production, eight 27ft-long flat-floor Lodekkas with the designation LDS (including three with convertible open-top bodywork) were supplied to a new Lodekka customer, Brighton Hove and District.

Two prototype forward-entrance Lodekkas, again with completely flat floors on the lower saloon and air suspension at the rear, also appeared in 1959-60. The first was a 30ft long FLF type (Flat floor, Long wheelbase, Forward entrance) with 70-seat bodywork, which joined Bristol Omnibus Company (as the operating Bristol company had been renamed) as fleet number LC8540 (995 EHW). The second was a short wheelbase, 27ft 6in long FSF type with 60-seat body which entered service with West Yorkshire as DX 82 (YWW 77). Both vehicles had sliding air-operated entrance doors when new, as did a small number of FLFs built subsequently for Thames Valley, through 4-leaf electrically-operated jackknife doors became standard for most production forward entrance Lodekkas. The new range of double-deckers from Bristol therefore consisted of the forward entrance FLF and FSF types which were complemented by two equivalent rear entrance Lodekka models, the FL and FS, which were similar to the LDX types of 1958. Both the FLF and FL types had a wheelbase of 19ft 2in, which was 8in longer than the six LDL vehicles produced three years earlier. As in the case of earlier models, the code '6B' or '6G' followed the chassis type letters to denote the number of cylinders and engine builder's initial — B for Bristol, G for Gardner.

The popularity of the different F-series Lodekka models varied considerably, leading to the FL and FSF types being dropped by 1963 so very few of either model received the revised design of grille introduced for Lodekkas the previous year. Only 45 FL chassis were ever built, two of which joined Western SMT while the others were shared between Eastern Counties, Hants & Dorset, Lincolnshire and Red & White. The FSF was a little more popular with production totalling 218, though Central SMT was the only Scottish operator attracted to this type.

The FS perpetuated the original LD concept

Left:
From 1962 Lodekkas were fitted with a revised front grille which incorporated the model name at the bottom and allowed for the fitment of a rectangular number plate in place of the square type used previously. This is a 1962 FS6G of Red & White Services of Chepstow. *J. White*

and found favour with many operators, nearly 900 being produced from 1960 to 1966. Among Tilling companies with the largest FS fleets were Crosville, Eastern Counties, Hants & Dorset, United Counties and West Yorkshire while 100 FSs were supplied north of the border, divided between Alexander (Fife), Central SMT, Scottish Omnibuses and Western SMT.

Of the later Lodekkas, however, the model produced in the greatest quantity was the FLF which was purchased in large numbers by Bristol Omnibus, Eastern National, Southern & Western National, United Auto and, in Scotland, Central SMT. In addition, sizeable FLF fleets could be found with Crosville, Eastern Counties, Hants & Dorset, Midland General and Mansfield District, Scottish Omnibuses, Thames Valley, United Counties and Western SMT. Over 1,800 FLFs were built before production ceased in 1968, including 179 31ft-long models with extended rear overhangs which were allocated to Alexander (Fife), Central SMT, Eastern National and Eastern Scottish. The last FLF built was, however, a standard model which became Midland General 313 (YNU 351G).

Bristol's own engines or Gardner 6LW or 6LX units were used to power most Lodekkas (with Leyland engines being employed in a few cases) while four- or five-speed crash gearboxes remained standard throughout the model's production life, although semi-automatic transmission became an option in later years.

New Bristol Lodekkas were only ever supplied to nationalised Tilling or Scottish bus undertakings, although when released from sales restrictions in 1965 Bristol proposed further variants to broaden the model's appeal

Right:
This view of a 1965 FLF with Gardner engine for Central SMT illustrate key features of the Lodekka — the low frame, the offset drive-line and the drop-centre rear axle. Note also the fuel tank, designed to occupy the space under the stairs. *Bristol*

on the open market. However, these plans came to nothing due largely to the growing demand for one-man operation for which, of course, the Lodekka with its front-mounted engine and separate cab was not at all suited (despite some brave attempts by Eastern National to prove otherwise by the conversion of several FLFs for omo with the driver taking fares across the rear area of the bonnet).

The Lodekka could, nevertheless, be found in use with municipalities and non-state-owned companies in the form of the Dennis Loline — which was the Lodekka built under licence by Dennis of Guildford. Indeed, some of the last of these actually had rear axles displaying Bristol badges. Over 280 Dennis Lolines, with forward or rear entrance bodywork, were constructed, though this model never enjoyed the popularity of the true Bristol product. Also less successful were a host of rival front-engined lowheight chassis which followed from other manufacturers, but none of which ever achieved the production volume of the Bristol design.

With over 5,200 Lodekkas constructed, this model was eventually replaced by the rear-engined Bristol VRT, which was also available in lowheight form, and later still by the rear-engined Bristol-built B45 — which became better known as the Leyland Olympian. Although no longer built at Bristol, the Olympian, with dropped-centre rear axle and low chassis frame designed to be closely integrated with the bodywork, displays several features derived from the Lodekka. In perpetuating Bristol's lowheight double-decker concept it can be seen as a direct descendant of the original Lodekka design of 1949.

Table 2: Lodekka dimensions

Model type	Length ft in	Width ft in	Wheelbase ft in	Normal seating capacity
LDX001/2	26′ 0″	7′ 6″	15′ 11″	58
LD	27′ 0″	8′ 0″	16′ 9″	58/60
LDL	30′ 0″	8′ 0″	18′ 6″	70
FS	27′ 4″	8′ 0″	16′ 11″	60
FSF	27′ 6″	8′ 0″	16′ 11″	60
FL	30′ 0″	8′ 0″	19′ 2″	70
Standard FLF	30′ 0″	8′ 0″	19′ 2″	70
Extra long FLF	31′ 1″	8′ 0″	19′ 2″	78

Below:
The forward-entrance Lodekkas had a more upright front profile. A 1964 FLF6G in the Western SMT fleet illustrates the later style of grille used on Lodekkas.
Stewart J. Brown

Right:
Eastern Counties was one of the last NBC fleets to operate Lodekkas. This 1967 FLF is seen in Cambridge in 1981.
Stewart J. Brown

Marks & Spence
Bovis
NTH ARBURY
185
Marks & Spen
We regret th
inconvenienc
during
rebuilding
FLF464
KAH 464D
EASTERN COUNTIES
193

Alan Millar

Tender stakes tame the wayward child

The 1980s have seen some remarkable changes in the provision of London's bus services. Alan Millar takes a critical look at what has been happening.

In its latter years, London Transport behaved in a fashion more likely to be expected from a spoiled child.

It had little difficulty in getting the pocket money it needed for its expensive lifestyle, it protested loudly if asked too many questions about what it was doing, and when its toys (eg off-the-peg buses of the 1970s) failed to perform as it expected, it then threw them out of its toy box and demanded new ones.

That stroppy behaviour was being tempered by the end of the 1970s, as Conservative and Labour Greater London Council administrations exercised more control over LT, but much still needed to be done when LT was taken over in June 1984 by London Regional Transport, a State-owned organisation created in part so that it was easier for the Thatcher Government to abolish its hated GLC.

A new structure of control of London's public transport system became effective with that move, for LRT was more than just a nationalised LT. The public transport planning responsibilities of the GLC were taken over, too, and these formed the nucleus of an overall central management function at LRT. The bus, Underground and vehicle engineering businesses were turned into autonomous units, with new subsidiaries taking them over in April 1985. London Buses Ltd took over bus operation and Bus Engineering Ltd became responsible for heavy overhaul work carried out at the Chiswick and Aldenham works.

The new organisation was given a tough remit to control its expensive lifestyle. From relying on over £300 million a year in revenue support from ratepayers and taxpayers, it was given three years to get that figure below £100 million and reduce its unit costs by at least 2.5% a year in real terms.

For bus operation, it meant pressing ahead faster with measures which had begun to be adopted. The expensive overhaul procedures, by which buses were periodically stripped down and rebuilt in a fashion known in few other British bus undertakings, came under scrutiny. London Buses' garages were usually capable of

Right:
Few of the LRT contracts have been won on the basis of using new vehicles. A remarkable exception is the 283, won by Scancoaches using Jonckheere-bodied Scania K92s. *C. Drew*

Right:
Eastern National took over operation of the W9 and promptly gave it a new image as the 'W-Niner'. The service had previously been operated by Bristol LH buses; Eastern National introduced Wadham Stringer-bodied Bedfords with dual-purpose seating. *Peter Rowlands*

achieving similar results without tying up expensive assets like Chiswick and Aldenham. It took no more than two years for Aldenham to be discarded.

One-person operation, adopted less rapidly in London than elsewhere in Britain where traffic conditions are more civilised, became an objective for most, perhaps even all, of the route network. That meant keeping the last few hundred Daimler Fleetline double-deckers, expensive toys it had been throwing out of its box for the previous five years into the welcoming hands of less choosy operators. Its ageing Routemasters, ideal central London crowd shifters, but expensive to crew and maintain, were targeted for replacement over a five-year period.

Added to all this, but a fundamental feature of the new regime, was the legal requirement of LRT to seek competitive tenders for the operation of its bus services. In earlier years, London bus routes had been taken over by private operators in times of difficulty for LT, and more recently Surrey County Council had transferred subsidies from LT to London Country Bus Services on grounds of LCBS (the National Bus Company subsidiary formed in 1970 to take over LT's country services) offering better value for money. Now, LRT was to take this on to a much greater scale by offering three-year contracts for the operation of an increasing proportion of the network according to strict quality standards laid down by its planners.

The idea was that LRT would remain responsible for the marketing and timetabling of the services, and that it would collect all the fares paid on them. The contractor would provide buses which met LRT's standards, would operate according to LRT's schedules and would be paid an agreed sum for its pains. Given that London Buses' costs are widely acknowledged to be among the highest in the country, it looked like a recipe for a rapid thinning down of the traditional red double-deck fleet running in the capital.

Yet that was not the result of the allocation of the first round of 12 tenders, announced in

Left:
Not all LRT contracts were won by other operators; several were retained by London Buses including the H2 on which is seen Carlyle-bodied Ford Transit F529. *C. Drew*

Above:
Eastern National has been particularly successful in gaining LRT contracts, and has opened an operating base at Walthamstow, Leyland National 1801 (TJN 500R) is seen on service 206 at Woodford Bridge. *R. Hefford*

April 1985 and brought into effect from about three months later. The group of isolated suburban routes was carved very neatly, six staying with London Buses, the other six going to outsiders. Of the latter, NBC's London Country took over two (one to be worked by its coaching subsidiary, National London; the other a route it lost a few years before to LT) and Eastern National took over two. Two independents, Len Wright Travel and Crystals of Orpington, got the others.

Service improvements built into the package increased mileage by 2.5%, but savings of £750,000 flowed from the more efficient working methods adopted by London Buses and the other successful tenderers. Eastern National's

Below:
One of London Country's gains in 1986 was the Hampstead Hoppa, operated by a fleet of Mercedes-Benz minibuses. *Peter Rowlands*

two routes included the W9, a local service in the Enfield area which had been started as an experimental LT minibus route in the early 1970s, but which had grown to use 39-seat Bristol LHs. Eastern National took it down a size, to use shortened Bedford midibuses and generated new interest in the service by giving the buses their own 'W-Niner' livery. A year later, its other route in this batch was doubled in frequency and operated with Ford Transit minibuses instead of double-deckers.

The independents adopted different methods. Len Wright, having had a tender bid for the use of new single-deckers turned down, opted instead to replace the red London Buses Leyland Nationals on its 81 (Slough-Hounslow) route with broken LT toys in the shape of Daimler Fleetlines withdrawn after only seven years' service in London. Like the NBC buses on tendered routes, they were fitted with 'London Regional Transport Service' boards at the front, and BEL's services were called upon to provide LRT-standard destination equipment. The effect, when combined with the yellow-and-brown livery adopted by Wright, was to suggest a special wing of LRT and not a private company.

Crystals, committed to using smaller buses, started running the 146 route from Bromley to Downe in Kent with assorted mini- and midibuses until two HTI Maxeta-bodied Leyland Cubs were delivered new early in 1986.

Crystals already operated a local service in the Orpington area, but Len Wright was new to the stage bus business, although he had already established an enviable reputation for operation in the quality end of the coach market. In common with the other contracted operators, the independents used electronic ticket machines supplied by LRT, partly to standardise accounting, but also to help LRT use the information to plan future service developments.

LRT wasted little time in seeking tenders for more of its peripheral services, and over the second half of 1985 it sought bids for the operation of 24 more routes, including several which extended beyond the old GLC area into Essex, Surrey and Hertfordshire. In the cases of some of these, the counties sought separate tenders for the sections within their boundaries.

Left:
Among the first batch of tendered routes was the Hounslow to Slough service which was won by Len Wright trading as London Buslines and using former DMSs repainted in an eye-catching yellow livery. *A. L. Millar*

Left:
A lot happened in Orpington in 1986. Another independent to take over a former London service using former London buses was Metrobus, again using DMSs.
Peter Rowlands

If the first group of tenders had looked to some like a rather neat carve-up between the different operators, these later tenders were anything but. Out of the 24 routes, London Buses was successful in winning only eight, one of which was only part of an existing route. It could console itself that it also won back from London Country a New Barnet-St Albans service subsidised by Hertfordshire. But it suffered sorely overall, with its Loughton garage in Essex losing six of its seven routes to other operators and being left to close. It was probably rather less distressed to lose its Hertfordshire-supported Potters Bar minibus service to the independent North Mymms Coaches, for with that service also went its troublesome fleet of Dodge 50-Series minibuses.

The two NBC companies which did best in the first round went on to consolidate their gains. Eastern National, which established a Citybus division for LRT routes and drafted in Bristol VRT double-deckers from other parts of its empire, got seven more routes around the Walthamstow and Ilford areas, while London Country won tenders for six more routes, most of them around the southwest of London, and retained a Cheam-Warlingham service it already operated with LRT support.

London Country's gains also included the 268 Hampstead local service, which LRT wanted to convert from Leyland National to higher frequency minibus operation. In its new hands, Mercedes-Benz minibuses were used, operated from a London Country minibus base at the Scratchwood service area on the M1. Minibuses used on a London Country service in Boreham Wood are run from the same base.

For its more conventional service gains, London Country went on a buying spree, building up a fleet of second-hand Leyland Atlantean double-deckers. It started with eight Park Royal-bodied examples from Southdown — ideal because they had three-track rear number displays suitable for LRT's requirement of front and rear displays — and followed this with 11 similar buses from Northern General. But for another 31 buses (and the option of more), it went out of NBC to Strathclyde PTE for surplus Alexander-bodied Atlanteans with side number displays. They and other LCBS buses on tendered routes showed rear numbers on slot-in boards.

The deal with Strathclyde completed a circle of Anglo-Scottish bus sales. London Buses, losing out in the tender battles, was selling Routemasters to the Scottish Bus Group for use in competition with Strathclyde's buses in Glasgow. Now, Strathclyde was selling redundant vehicles to one of the companies most successful in hurting London Buses.

Independents won the rest. Len Wright gained another route in the Hounslow area, Ensign Bus (the operating wing of the dealership which bought most of LT's surplus Fleetlines) shared a Dagenham area route with Eastern National, Cityrama (the London sightseeing tour operator) won authority for an inter-suburban South London route (200), Sampson Travel of Hoddesdon won the tender for a route from Enfield as well as winning some Essex tenders, and Scancoaches (a quality coach operator) won the tender for the 283 route in West London.

Scancoaches, owned by Finns and already standardised on Scania and Volvo coaches, bought five Scania K92 single-deckers with Jonckheere Trans-City two-door bodies for its service and decked them out with front, side

Above:
A new London Buses subsidiary, Orpington Buses, was set up to operate small buses on tendered routes around the town. It uses the Roundabout fleetname as shown on this 1986 Optare CityPacer, based on a MAN-VW LT55 chassis. Orpington Buses had five CityPacers and 24 Ivecos when it started operating. *Peter Rowlands*

and rear destination displays operated electrically. The others all chose the ubiquitous ex-LT Fleetlines which, by now, were beginning to make LRT feel as silly as it looked. If others were winning tenders with them, then why had LT sold them?

London Buses, which was struggling to sell its labour force the idea of lower wage rates in the suburbs to combat competition for tenders, won three of the West London tenders by the device of creating a separate subsidiary company, Stanwell Buses, to run with its own terms and conditions of employment. A fleet of dedicated buses, all Leyland Nationals, was allocated to the new company and operated with 'Westlink' fleetnames and LRT contract plates on the front.

Another separate company, Orpington Buses, was also successful in winning tenders in 1986 for the operation of much of a recast local service network in North Kent. This company, trading as Roundabout, bought its own fleet of 30 Robin Hood-bodied Iveco Daily and Optare City Pacer-bodied Volkswagen midibuses for use on five new services and an Orpington area service which Crystals had been operating before 1985. Independent Metrobus (with even

Right:
Ensign, well known as the dealer of DMSs, now runs DMSs on LRT services, including the 145, on which is B212 on its first day of operation, 21 June 1986. *R. Hefford*

Sampson was yet another independent who showed that the DMSs were not quite so bad as London Transport had made out. This one is seen in 1986 at Waltham Abbey. *Peter Rowlands*

Crystals of Orpington took over the 146 service and bought new buses for it. These were Leyland Cubs, a model more commonly associated with welfare buses and rarely seen as the basis of a PSV. The angular bodywork was by HTI. *A. L. Millar*

more ex-LT Fleetlines) added two routes to others already run in the area, London Country another.

But this was only a foretaste of the way that LRT saw the future shape of the Capital's buses. In its first tranche of tenders for operation from 1987, the process was swung into central London. Of nine routes put out to tender in June 1986, three penetrated the heart of London and part of one was to be converted into a high frequency minibus route.

So keen was LRT to impose standards on the operation of tendered minibus routes, that it ordered 40 more City Pacers — the first urban minibus developed from the start as a bus and not as a converted bread van — which it would lease to successful winners of its tenders.

The first were leased to London Buses for use on a tourist service linking Parliament Square with Kensington, while others were earmarked for an ambitious plan to convert part of the 53 route between Oxford Circus and Parliament Hill Fields into a heavily publicised 2½-4min frequency service.

If this was to be the shape of things to come, it would be a crippling blow to the ailing British bus manufacturing industry, for the tendering process had already frozen London Buses' big bus ordering plans following the supply of 260 Leyland Olympians in 1986. Double-deckers, already expensive to build for a declining market, could become a decreasingly attractive proposition to manufacturers deprived of the opportunity of being suppliers to Britain's biggest customer for the breed.

For the public, the initial experience of LRT tendering was working well. The same service, even a better service in many cases, has been provided for less subsidy; new ideas have been applied to the operation of the route network; and London Buses has been made to behave less extravagantly. The spoiled child is growing up fast into a responsible adult.

Below:
London Country scored considerable successes in tendering in 1986 and 1987 and had to buy additional double-deck buses to cope. These included former Strathclyde PTE Leyland Atlantean AN68s with panoramic-windowed Alexander bodywork. This one is seen in North Cheam. *A. L. Millar*

John Aldridge

Down under

John Aldridge reviews the Australian bus business, finding much of interest to European enthusiasts.

Are there many English buses there? your editor asked, when I suggested an article about Australian buses. 'Yes' I replied with the confidence of one keen to write an article. To be more correct, as said editor is a Scot, he probably said British buses.

Either way, it really depends on quite what you mean. There are both 'British' British buses there; for example, a Northern Counties-bodied Bristol VR 'Jumbo' ex-Reading Corporation, now in Melbourne, and there are also British Australian buses there, in the shape of numerous Australian bodied Bedfords and Leylands. Brisbane boasts the world's largest fleet of Leyland Panthers, nearly all of them still running when I was there. But their locally-built bodies make them look totally different.

On the coach side you can find second-hand imported Plaxton or Duple-bodied Bedfords or Leylands, looking exactly as they would in the UK, and sometimes just as anonymous too, like the one I found at Sydney Airport. And another double-decker in Melbourne is, I think, an Alexander-bodied Fleetline ex-City of Oxford.

Below:
Melbourne reinstated some elderly AEC Regal VIs — this one is seen in the city centre against a backdrop of trams.

Above:
The world's biggest fleet of Leyland Panthers is to be found in Brisbane. Angled flat-glass windscreens give the driver good visibility while minimising reflections.

You can find many more non-British products too, for the Europeans are there in force with Mercedes, MAN, Volvo and Scania, plus DAF and Renault (if you look hard and are in the right place), and plenty of Japanese — mainly Hinos.

When I say you can find, finding isn't that easy. Australia is huge, bigger than Western Europe, as big as the United States, and even to cross it by air from east to west (or vice versa) takes over 5hr.

So even the holiday of a lifetime, with plenty of money to spend on travel and accommodation, would have to be tempered with some sort of plan and aims. After all, you wouldn't try to visit Spain, Portugal, France, Holland, Belgium, Germany, Austria and Italy all in one go, would you?

But if it's as big as Europe or the US, it certainly hasn't the population. That totals a modest 15 million. And, of course, the fewer the people, the fewer the buses. Most of the population lives near the coast, and in particular within about 50 miles of the east coast, where you have (reading downwards) Brisbane, Sydney and Melbourne relatively close together, followed by Adelaide on the south coast. But the distances are considerable: Brisbane-Sydney by air is 472 miles (755km), Sydney-Melbourne is 453 miles (725km), and Melbourne-Adelaide is 409 miles (655km). By road, and the way the coaches go, the mileages are greater: Greyhound offers Brisbane-Sydney via the New England Highway in 17hr for the 722-mile (1,175km) journey, or in 15hr via the Pacific Highway for the 637 mile (1,020km) journey. There's the capital, Canberra, between Sydney and Melbourne, and then there's Perth on the far west coast. In between, an awful lot of sparsely populated country, and often dirt roads.

Naturally, the rarer or more exotic vehicles tend to be with smaller operators in more remote places, often being used mainly on the inevitable school runs. So even an ardent enthusiast would find it hard to cover the country in the way that can be done in the UK.

One feature that makes Australia different is the strength of the individual states. Australia was not a British colony, it was several. Today individual states are still surprisingly powerful, and there is 'state preference' which allows contracts to be placed with the best local builder, even if his tender is 10% higher than the lowest tender from another state.

So the new Mercedes used on the new guided busway in Adelaide were not assembled in the Mercedes assembly plant in Sydney. No, they were put together by — wait for it — Mitsubishi Motors Australia, and bodies too were locally produced by PMC (Adelaide). A bodybuilder may have more than one assembly plant, but in different states. One cannot imagine Perth buying buses completed in Melbourne or Sydney, some 2,700 miles (4,330km) away. But good second-hand buys, such as last-forever Leyland Worldmasters, do make the journey eastwards in later life to new homes.

The other odd thing about manufacturers is ownership. A large, but independent, organisation is JRA Ltd, and J stands for Jaguar and R for Rover. As well as involvement in cars (including other makes) it owns PMC (Pressed Metal Corporation), Adelaide and Pressed Metal, Sydney, and distributes Hinos through Hino Bus Australia (with assembly in Sydney and Adelaide) and Denning.

A list of chassis makes more-or-less currently available would include Austral, Bova, DAF, Denning, Elwood, Hino, IBC, International, Isuzu, Kia, Leyland, MAN, MCA, Mitsubishi, Mercedes, Nissan, Renault, Scania, Setra, Volgren, and Volvo. A list of bodybuilders would be even longer.

Heat and dust make Australian operating conditions tough, particularly for coaches. The long distances add another dimension, too. The general manager of the quaintly named Kangaroo Flat Bus Lines in Bendigo (near Melbourne) told me that changing to a premium specification oil meant that the Hinos which regularly take school parties to Alice Springs (in the middle of Australia) could now do the round trip without an oil change. Previously the driver himself had to do one at Alice Springs.

Enthusiasts have to be very careful in identifying buses too. Resourceful operators a long way from supply lines, rebuild or change units or move engines: front, mid and rear engined Bedfords are all common, though they might not have been built like that, and they might well not have a Bedford engine. My Kangaroo Flat friend has a Scania-engined Hino.

Below:
A Melbourne AEC Regal IV in the new yellow and green livery which was normally applied only to more modern buses. *J. M. Aldridge*

Above:
Melbourne-Brighton Bus Lines ran a mainly Leyland fleet including four dual-door Freighter-bodied Panthers. This one is seen after the take over by the Metropolitan Transit Authority.

The most unlikely PSVs are based on Mercedes Unimog chassis, and are used to carry tourists in the outback beyond Alice Springs and Ayers Rock. The Unimog is a four-wheel drive vehicle with a flexing chassis which enables it to cope with rough terrain and is widely used by farmers and the military.

The average visitor is likely to spend more of his time in and around the major cities, so Sydney is the obvious fleet to start with. Its municipal fleet (the Urban Transit Authority of New South Wales) runs about 1,700 vehicles in the cities of Sydney and Newcastle — the latter is about a 2½-hr coach ride north of Sydney. It has bought Mercedes rear-engined buses in recent years, which boast four different body types. Some of the newest are artics, which have generally ousted the last double-deckers, Leyland Atlanteans. When I was there Atlanteans still survived on one route, to Palm Beach, which included a not particularly severe hairpin bend, round which, said the unions, artics were dangerous. Unfortunately the Atlanteans finally bowed out a few months later, in mid-1986. Older Sydney buses are varieties of Leyland Leopard.

The Atlanteans once numbered 200, with rather crude-looking PMC bodies, which brings me to another point. Axle weights are much more restricted in much of Australia, so crude-looking bodywork on pre- or postwar double-deckers, or high capacity buses, can be a matter almost of necessity, rather than poor design. Rear overhang of rear-engined buses is noticeably shorter than in Europe, and Sydney also has some particularly strange Mercedes artics: they have no doors in the rear section, though two in the front.

A rather smaller bus fleet can be found in Melbourne, though compensation is provided in the shape of the fascinating tram fleet which still includes numerous 1930s Australian style ones as well as more recent Scandinavian-based designs. Famous Flinders Street boasts numerous trams, plus private and ex-private buses and municipal ones — and crowds of passengers.

Not long before I arrived in Melbourne there had been a long and complicated dispute involving one of the best known private operators in the area, Melbourne-Brighton Bus

Lines. They sold out to the municipal or state operator, but drivers then apparently refused to drive some of the buses, which were not fitted with power steering. This led to Melbourne's Metropolitan Transit Authority dusting off some strange and long-stored AEC Regal Mark VIs (they were an Australian model). Strange because they had been built when there were restrictions on the number of passengers a one-man bus could carry; so they had short bodies, the shortening being done by having hardly any body behind the rear axle. Some of them had subsequently been narrowed too: Melbourne has an 8ft 6in width limit to which they had been built. When a dealer was hoping to dispose of some elsewhere, he narrowed them so that they were suitable for private operators elsewhere, but not all were sold, and some narrow ones also went back into service.

What's more, owing to a misunderstanding at the depot, one or two boasted the latest MTA livery of mid-green and 'gold' — mid-green and bright orange would be a better description. The depot decided to repaint one or two of the scruffiest, and ordered the old paints; the stores man thought they meant the new image colours, so having got the paint they painted them in the new style . . .

If Leyland Panthers are your favourite bus, you can find them still. The Melbourne-Brighton had some which went to the MTA, some small operators have them, and then there's Brisbane. On Mondays to Fridays and Saturday mornings you can find vast numbers of them in Brisbane, a city higher up the east coast and whose climate is rather more humid than Sydney's.

Brisbane is also trying artics in some numbers and has several one-offs; for example one Scania, and one DAF, plus a fleet of Volvos that were used in Japan in 1985 for Expo 85 at Tsukuba. All told there were 100 of these Volvos, all with Japanese-built bodies by Fuji Heavy Industries. Volvo Australia subsequently imported quite a number, some of which have been sold to private bus companies. The Japanese Volvos have coach seating, of attractive colours, with groups of different seats in different colours. They have been Australianised in rather strange fashion in Brisbane, with one doorway being filled in rather crudely. The ex-Japanese artics are said

Below:
The last generation of Australian double-deckers were 224 Leyland Atlanteans with PMC bodies for the Department of Government Transport. They were delivered in the early 1970s. The peak hour express service from Sydney to Palm Beach was their last route, worked by a handful of survivors until mid-1986. Many of these buses are now with private operators.

Above:
Tourist operations feature a number of second-hand double-deckers. This ex-Reading Transport Northern Counties-bodied Bristol VRT is an unusual choice for an import. It is seen in Melbourne.

to have cost Aus $225,000 (about £112,000) new, and to have been bought by the Brisbane undertaking for about Aus $120,000 (£60,000).

Brisbane plans ultimately to go about 40% artic, but when I was there had these Japanese Volvos (six of them), plus two Autralian (Denning)-bodied Volvos, plus two MANs, plus the DAF already mentioned (with an Austral body) and the Scania, which is a 'pusher' with engine in the rear and a Denning body. Quite a mixture.

But then mixtures are common. What one can call the great move away from UK suppliers to European ones has seen some city undertakings go from first one make to another. Brisbane had some Leyland Nationals but went mainly to MAN. Melbourne went to Volvo first, after buying 30 Leyland Nationals, but after having 100 rear-engined Volvo B59s (not that common a vehicle worldwide) went on to buy 150 rear-engined MANs. And Adelaide, our next port of call, had a vast fleet of AEC Swifts, nearly 400 at one stage. Then came Volvo B59s (nearly 300 of them). Next were about 40 underfloor-engined Volvo B58 artics, followed by ordinary Volvo B58s, and then 140 rear-engined MANs.

But when Adelaide came to its guided busway, which without doubt is one of the major sights of Australian bus operation, it bought 90 Mercedes, some artic and some rigid. The busway, opened in 1986, is the world's longest. Once the route was planned as a motorway, then as a railway . . . or tramway, but political and environmental considerations led to the guided busway. Half is in use already, with at rush hours a bus a minute travelling at 60mph (100kmh), and the rest should be completed in 1988.

The busway runs out to north-east suburbs of Adelaide, and is used by some 10 routes. The attraction of the concrete busway was that the guidance system enables a much narrower roadway to be provided than with a conventional buses-only roadway as at Runcorn. The Adelaide buses continue their journeys at both ends on conventional roads.

Considerable variety is added to bus operations around Sydney, Melbourne and Brisbane by the private bus operators with what we would call stage services. They are particularly numerous in the outer areas of Sydney, a city whose urban sprawl is vast. That is because nearly everybody likes to (and can afford to) live in a house or bungalow with its own garden and swimming pool. An inter-city coach on which I travelled overnight from Melbourne to Sydney set down its first Sydney-bound passengers in the suburb of Liverpool at 7am, but it took another 2hr (and a few more stops) before we actually reached central Sydney. In these suburbs you will find numerous private operators, with a mixture of new and second-hand stock.

Most of Australia isn't city, so to conclude I will mention a visit to one of the larger (relatively speaking) centres in rural Queensland. Queensland is Australia's largest state, occupies the north-east part of the country, and is larger than Holland, Denmark, Belgium, West Germany, Switzerland, Italy, Spain and France put together. The town is Biloela, where the 21-vehicle fleet of Biloela Coaches is based.

Most of the fleet is on school work, but there are also contracts carrying workers some 18km (11 miles) to an electricity plant and, on these high-backed seats are a contractual requirement. 'A bit silly, but that's what they wanted', says the proprietor. One of the first things that strikes you about the fleet is its exceptional cleanliness, inside and out. But then they employ six cleaners, four of whom are 'casuals' working to midday only, and the other two also drive the school buses.

Most of the fleet is named. *Miss Biloela* is a 1969 Denning with Detroit Diesel engine; *June* is a small Bedford with Atholl Hedges body; *Miss Banana Shire* (there is a nearby town called Banana) is a 1985 GM-powered Denning coach; and *Pup* is a 25-seater, probably a Bedford, but I couldn't be sure. There are a number of Albion Vikings in the fleet, and what looked like a lesser Denning also boasted an Albion Viking steering wheel, which shows how careful one has to be in identifying buses.

Australian coaches generally are varied these days, with Volvos, Scanias, Mercedes and even Bovas on long-distance work, as well as home products. But there is one coach that is typical, common, universal . . . it's the Denning. Dennings, with Detroit Diesel two-stroke engines, are what made Australian coaching. They are rugged and reliable, if a bit too thirsty these days, but they stand up to the dirt roads, the high and low temperatures, the pollen and dust that gets everywhere. And everybody knows how to mend a Denning.

Below:
If there is one make which has put Australian coaching on the map it is the Denning with Detroit Diesel two-stroke engine. These two are laying over in Sydney.

Roger Kaye

The end of the road

Unlike old soldiers, old buses do die — although sometimes it is a lingering death. Roger Kaye illustrates vehicles in various stages of dereliction in Yorkshire scrapyards.

Below left:
The vantage point of an abandoned railway embankment in 1979 shows serried ranks of dead buses — London Transport Fleetlines and Merlins, Chesterfield Titans and a few oddities like the London Country ex-Ribble PD3 on the left. The shell in the foreground was a London Country Swift.

Bottom left:
There is something surrealistic about this view of an RT with its body stripped to the shell being driven at speed through a scrapyard in 1977 before having its engine removed and its body frame broken up.

Below:
Assorted abandoned RTs lean drunkenly in a breaker's yard in 1978.

Above left:
Before Routemasters became Desirable Property (see page 28) many followed the RTs to the Yorkshire breakers. This sad line was photographed in the spring of 1986.

Left:
'Batteries flat', is the message chalked above the fleet number of RM585. That would seem to be the least of its troubles in this 1986 view.

Below left:
1985 — and reflections of an ex-Colchester AEC Regent V with Massey body in a muddy yard.

Below:
Not all buses get dismantled gently. A mechanical grab tears an ex-Central SMT Bristol FLF apart in the spring of 1986. In the foreground a sea of wheels; behind abandoned seat frames conjure up images of a strange metal hedge.

Above right:
It may once have been one of Bassett's Luxury Coaches, but by 1985 this badly damaged Foden was waiting to be broken up.

Right:
An unusual find in a British scrapyard is an Irish Atlantean. This former CIE bus was photographed in May 1986.

Below:
It is rare to find really old buses in breakers' yards but these two Bristol Ks were approaching 40 years of age when photographed in 1986. They had highbridge ECW bodies and were new to Eastern Counties.

Mike Cornish

The Super National programme

Mike Cornish, who was responsible for the Special Vehicle Business of Leyland Truck & Bus from the mid-1970s, describes the development of non-standard Nationals.

Leyland Truck and Bus had launched the Leyland National single-deck city bus in 1971 and were moving forward with mixed success. The National was Britain's first production-line, volume-produced bus. It was of integral construction and was designed to have its fully-tooled pressed metal panels jig-assembled using non-craft labour. The disciplined strictures of pressed tool and jig assembly investment meant that the final product had a limited number of specification variations. Although the standard specification was to a higher level than operators had been used to, there were only four paint colours plus white in the 'on-line' automatic spray booth. Operators had been using traditional colours, passed down through the years and buses were generally brush painted. So what was a BS colour? And what was *spray* painting? All this was seen as limiting choice and led to a certain resistance to purchase.

At the same time there had been changes in vehicle layout. Operating fashions changed during the period between the start of planning and the formal launch of the Leyland National. When planning started only single-deckers could be used for one-man operation. By the time the Leyland National reached production, one-man double-deckers were commonplace. Sales volumes were not matching output and at this point I was given the brief 'to lift the image of buses in general and Leyland National in particular'.

Both public and operator perception of buses was poor. Buses were for the second-class citizen and the socially deprived, infirm or the very young and the Leyland National was take-it-or-leave-it: 'any colour you like so long as it's black' — except that Leyland did not offer this option.

To address the problem, Leyland researched and observed that the bus was actively discriminated against in favour of the motorcar. In 1973 I put together a paper called 'Planning for the Bus' which looked at ways of restoring the bus to its former efficient and fast 'People Mover'

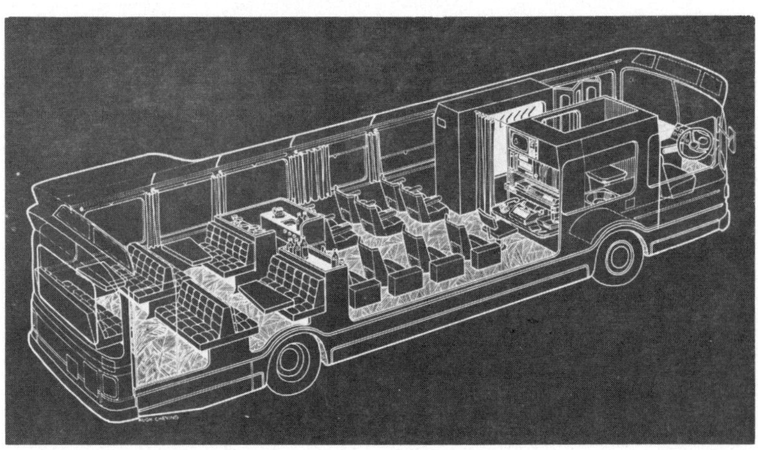

Right:
A cut-away drawing showing a possible layout for a Leyland National executive commuter coach. *Leyland*

Right:
The lavishly-equipped interior of a Super National. The individual seats were fitted with seat belts.
Leyland

role. This paper dealt with the actual role of the bus as a victim of the traffic scene and its potential role when incorporated in a planned transport system.

Leyland took a flyer at the Moving People in Cities exhibition for which my paper had been written and exhibited a Leyland National 11.3m-long citybus carrying the legends *Leyland Super National* and *Business Commuter*.

The vehicle was liveried in smart business grey and white, and had immaculate graphics as well as showing off fibreglass curtains peeping through tinted glass. Inside it was something else. The *Business Commuter* was shown with 21 seats divided between two areas: one for work, the other for hospitality. An all-female crew was uniformed to match the vehicle livery.

The interior of the vehicle was sumptuously furnished with heavy carpeting and solid teak fittings. The seats in the front section were in royal blue corduroy and cream leather whilst the hospitality seats at the rear were in chocolate and cream. The equipment and systems encompassed a secretarial unit complete with secretary, electric typewriter, dictation unit, intercom to each seat to relay telephone calls, a public address system and a radio paging unit to recall any occupants who might be away from the vehicle. They could also be used to advise regular passengers that the vehicle was going to collect them from their house or office in X minutes time. Other equipment included TV video recorder, digital clocks, four-channel FM radio to each seat, shaver points, a wardrobe and individual lamps and dimmer controls at each seat. Each work place had an adjustable seat with seatbelt and personal locker and work table.

In the hospitality area there was a fitted kitchenette with water, food, coffee and drinks facilities. Tables were also provided and so was an eight-track stereo music system. The *Business Commuter* also had other thoughtful

Above:
The Lifeliner with hovercraft. This National was ultimately rebuilt as a bus for Midland Red. *Leyland*

features such as a photocopier and a document shredder as well as being exceptionally well thermally insulated. It even had lamps under the entrance step to illuminate the ground.

The reaction to the *Business Commuter* at the Moving People in Cities exhibition was overwhelmingly enthusiastic. This was not a bus, and could this be a Leyland National? It received lavish publicity from the media and as a result Leyland, who had only built it for a two-day life during the exhibition, were encouraged to turn it into a runner. It went into service and stayed there for the next 10 years. During that time only air conditioning was added. The *Business Commuter* was used for a wide range of activities, many of a promotional nature. It played its part in winning the Dewar Trophy and the Design Council Award in 1974.

The National Bus Company board decided that they would like one to use for private hire. Their Super National was even more elaborate and included a toilet, fridge, colour TV, a generating set and a combustion water heater. The NBC Super National was equipped to work in three separate modes. In addition to the normal moving vehicle mode, where all the on-board systems were powered by the main engine and its storage battery packs, the vehicle could be parked and power could be supplied by the main engine, the generating set or, for longer duration stops, by plugging into the main commercial supply.

This and the earlier *Business Commuter* could be described as high profile vehicles and it was this high profile that attracted a lot of attention from the mass media. Both vehicles became the subject of feature articles in newspapers and magazines around the world. National and network TV took an interest. The *Business Commuter* even appeared on the BBC's *Blue Peter Show*. Public awareness was growing and our programme was beginning to work. People were beginning to call, saying 'If you can do that to a Leyland National, how about . . .?' The perceived rigidity of the Leyland National specification was being dismantled piece by piece, whilst the image of the standard bus was being uplifted.

The first two Super Nationals amounted to very high specification versions of a bus, but now it was time to look in other directions and to link the Leyland National through a process of metamorphosis with a new need. I was introduced to a doctor who was heavily engaged in a group providing prompt at-the-scene medical attention to accident victims. This group, known as DART, worked in the Doncaster and Rotherham area. One of their needs was for stabilisation and on-the-spot care for accident victims rather than always rushing them towards the nearest hospital. I began to formulate the idea of a major incident, casualty clearing, stabilisation and command control unit.

The scheme was to produce a mobile vehicle that would act as a receiving, stabilisation and treatment unit. It would be safe, secure and quiet. The floors would be level in spite of the terrain, with headroom approaching 2m.

The concept was named *Lifeliner*. The *Lifeliner* was designed as a self-contained unit with search and rescue capabilty as well as for patient care. The search and rescue role was aided by a go-anywhere vehicle, a stretcher-carrying machine with four-wheel drive and four-wheel steering which formed part of the *Lifeliner* kit. A lightweight hovercraft with a carrying capacity of four was roof-mounted on the *Lifeliner* during transportation. It was lowered to the ground via a chute which was like a shop sun blind with upturned sides to ensure directional accuracy during the descent. The *Lifeliner* carried 4,500 watts of flood-lighting on an elevating mast to illuminate the general area. There was a further 1,200 watts of lighting for the area inside and immediately around the *Lifeliner*. A winch with an eight-tonne line pull was fitted at the front of *Lifeliner* to assist with disentanglements.

Lifeliner acted as a central, on-site disaster management HQ. A single unit from which was controlled medical, fire, police and search and rescue services. This was new in 1974. *Lifeliner* had all the latest communications aids and its computers carried data about the locations of hazards such as chemical stores and their specific content.

Again the task was to achieve public awareness and it worked. I went for saturation coverage with the media. *Lifeliner* appeared in everything from the *Daily Telegraph* to *Nursing Mirror*, from *She* magazine to *Engineering in Medicine*. VIZ NEWS made a film and BBC TV did a feature for *Tomorrows World*.

Lifeliner again demonstrated that the Leyland National bus was anything but 'take-it-or-leave-it'. More orders accrued for the standard product to be used for bus operations, whilst

Below:
The original airside Nationals had a 'people scoop' at the front but were later rebuilt with conventional front entrances. These vehicles had a centre door on both sides of the body. *Leyland*

others were built to be turned into mobile bank branches.

Many of the features embodied in the Super Nationals were selected and engineered in such a way that they went through the Leyland manufacturing plant facilities, its drilling and assembly jigs, without disruption. Many of these features were to become integral parts of regular Leyland Nationals as well as the Super Nationals which followed.

In 1975 the first of the Airside Super Nationals was built, three of them, in conjunction with Wadham Stringer of Portsmouth. The most noticeable feature was the 'people scoop' at the front nearside where once just over half the windscreen had been. Double doors were fitted to bay five on both the left- and right-hand side of the vehicle. Perimeter seating was used and the saloon featured supplementary heating. Torque convertor transmissions were used for smooth starts, because of the large number of standees carried.

Hitherto it had been impossible to have a *three-door* Leyland National because of structural implications. The Airside project represented a breakthrough in that the structural changes needed could all be processed through the manufacturing plant without new investment. The 'people scoop' at the front end was discontinued for operational reasons and the vehicles were converted to a standard nearside doorway in the front overhang. Many subsequent Airside Super Nationals have had three doors.

The upshot of these activities was a call for further special vehicles. These included:

- Airside buses for a variety of people
- Oil riggers' express
- Health Authority staff transit 62-seater in lieu of the regular 52
- Category 'A' prisoner transit
- Product training vehicle
- Driver training vehicle
- Police transit
- Exhibition units

Generally throughout the programme I managed to keep the Leyland National bus largely within its original format and dimensions. It was only aspects of the *Lifeliner* and the 'people scoop' on Airside buses which represented any departure from that policy.

Below:
The oil riggers' express had a raised flat floor and combined the long front bays of the 11.3m bus with the short rear bays of the 10.3m model. It operated for Rennie of Dunfermline. *Leyland*

A spin-off from the Super National programme was the C27 project which offered a National understructure with an Eastern Coach Works body which would be suitable for overseas assembly. *Leyland*

The next and very brief programme plan was to look at what else I could do to a Leyland National to increase production. In cases where the whole vehicle could not be sold, could part of it?

I looked at using the bodyshell in trimmed or untrimmed form. Could I make it into an exhibition trailer by putting a kingpin under the engine bearers and using a height-adjusted axle in the second bay? With this arrangement the whole lot would effectively go backwards with an articulated tractor unit doing the work. There were economic strengths and weaknesses with this concept. I passed over this one, and left it for a rainy day, turning instead to concept changes with greater implications.

I suppose that what came next was really a development of the 'if I can't sell all of it' philosophy. British Rail's fleet of Diesel Multiple Units was life-expired. BR had an obligation to provide service and their fleet was expensive to maintain. Replacement on a like-for-like basis was unthinkable and the exotic and expensive Class 210 solution even more unthinkable.

BR's Transport Technology Assessment Group had been studying small vehicles for lightly used rural services. They were finding it difficult to make progress. Their work led them to write to Leyland to ask if bus production techniques were a possibility. I responded saying that not just techniques could be used but specific parts, jigs and fixtures of an existing design. It was no good being more or less the same, they had to be identical. Any change would incur a cost penalty while no change represented a compromise compared with the clean sheet ideal solution. However, the compromise was not a deterrent when viewed against what a redesign might cost.

With a brief specification from TTAG comprising largely length, width and height dimensions, we applied the Leyland standard modular interpretation. TTAG saw their study as just considering small vehicles while I saw it as an opportunity which, when converted into production hardware, could be the basis of a BR DMU replacement. This I did, and thus was born the Leyland Experimental Vehicle (LEV), the first Super National rail vehicle, more commonly known as The Railbus.

The LEV ran on a modified two-axle rail freight chassis and was followed by bigger and better versions initially using standard width Leyland National bodies. However, BR required two-plus-three seating, which led to the creation of the current successful wide-bodied Class 142 two-car units of which there are now 96 in operation — but that, as they say, is another story.

John Burnett

After the Atlantean

Production of the Leyland Atlantean ceased in 1986. John Burnett considers its successors.

The Atlantean was a hard act for Leyland to follow; it had not only been highly successful commercially but had brought about the rewriting of the conventions of bus design — and in the process had helped to give Leyland a monopoly of the double-deck bus market in Britain.

Leyland's competitors in this market at the time of the Atlantean launch — AEC, Guy, Bristol, Daimler and Dennis — either deserted the market or came under the wing of what ended up as British Leyland's Truck and Bus Division.

Wisely Leyland introduced the Atlantean to the market with a much more conventional specification than the original prototypes — a beam front axle, leaf spring suspension, body-on-chassis construction and a straight rear axle had replaced the more adventurous

Below:
Titan production started at Park Royal in 1978 and was transferred to Workington in 1980. Out of 1,169 production Titans built, 1,125 went to London Transport. Here a Titan passes an ECW-bodied Leyland Olympian in Whitehall.

features on the integral prototypes. But that was in 1958.

During the early 1970s Leyland developed the B15, later to be named Titan, a design which reinstated many of the features lost from the original Atlantean prototype — integral construction, independent front suspension and a dropped-centre rear axle. The Titan was a completely new design, however, and with London Transport as one of the main target customers (though not as much of a main customer as it turned out) the Titan could be thought of as just as much a descendant of the rear-engined Routemaster as of the Atlantean. The Titan was a very sophisticated bus — by the time Leyland were able to deliver in quantity the market had become much smaller, more competitive and, perhaps most important of all,

Top:
In 1982 Leyland built a Titan demonstrator. It failed to convince any operators that Titan's merits were worth the extra cost and was sold to Scottish operator Ian Glass of Haddington.

Right:
The Olympian was altogether a different kettle of fish, although many of its features were derived from the Titan. In 16ft 3in wheelbase form with Gardner engine and ECW body it became the standard NBC double-decker. This is a Crosville example in Chester.

Above:
The 18ft 6in wheelbase model has been specified by a minority of operators, including Lothian Region who are also unusual in specifying Leyland TL11 engines. The short bay amidships shows where extra length has been added to the ECW body. This one is seen loading beneath the castle in Edinburgh's Princes Street.

more cost-conscious. Production of the Titan ceased in 1984.

The 1980 Motor Show saw the unveiling of the Olympian underframe. As a separate chassis it could be fitted with independent bodywork, although this had to contribute to the stiffness of the vehicle structure. The Olympian was intended as the replacement for the Atlantean, Fleetline and Bristol VR and indeed was first produced at Bristol. There is no doubt that the Olympian, now produced in Leyland, is a success. Over 2,000 have been built.

In response to the success of the Volvo Citybus, Leyland caused some surprise by launching an underfloor-engined double-decker of its own, the Lion. The Tiger chassis was

Below:
London tried three experimental Olympians, one of which is seen here, before ordering 260 which were delivered in 1986-87.

Right:
The mid-engined Lion is of Danish descent, being built by DAB. The first examples were delivered in 1986 to Eastern Scottish and to Nottingham City Transport. The Eastern Scottish vehicles had Alexander R-type bodies with coach seats and an improved front end design; the Nottingham buses, one of which is shown here, were bodied by Northern Counties to that operator's unusual design.

perhaps the more obvious choice as the basis for such a model but Leyland's then Danish subsidiary, DAB, produced a lower chassis which was more suitable and it is from there that the Lion is imported, although of course major components such as the TL11H engine are British-built. The first Lions entered service with Eastern Scottish in the spring of 1986.

And the Atlantean? Production ceased towards the end of 1986 with one of the last, for the Kuwait Transport Company, being shown at that year's Motor Show.

Below:
The last built-up Atlanteans went to Kuwait and had Northern Counties bodies. This vehicle marked the Atlantean's last appearance at a Motor Show; it was on Northern Counties stand at the NEC in 1986. The last examples to enter service, in 1987, were built from kits shipped to Indonesia.

The *Buses Annual* 1988 quiz

1. **Which was the first NBC bus company to be privatised in 1986?:**
   a Badgerline
   b Devon General
   c Southern Vectis

2. **The main ex-NBC company serving Wigan is:**
   a Ribble
   b North Western
   c Crosville

3. **When did East Staffordshire District Council cease operating buses?:**
   a 1985
   b 1986
   c 1983

4. **The first Leyland Lynx in Great Britain was bought by:**
   a Halton
   b AA Motor Services
   c West Midlands

5. **United Transport's first English minibus operation started in:**
   a Greater Manchester
   b West Yorkshire
   c South Yorkshire

6. **Approximately how many buses did NBC run at the end of 1985 before privatisation was started?:**
   a 14,500
   b 13,600
   c 12,900

7. **Who bought the last open-platform double-decker in Britain?:**
   a Northampton
   b Blackpool
   c Stockport

8. **The first Leyland Olympian to enter service did so with:**
   a Ribble
   b Greater Manchester
   c Alexander (Midland)

9. **The biggest British operator of Dennis Dominators is:**
   a Central Scottish
   b Leicester City Bus
   c South Yorkshire PTE

10. **The first operator of the Volvo Citybus was:**
    a Strathclyde PTE
    b Derby City Transport
    c Merseyside PTE

11. **The number of British operators to buy *double-deck* Dennis Falcons was:**
    a 1
    b 2
    c 4

12. **In the early 1980s Plaxton produced a coach body with shallow flat glass side windows. It was called the:**
    a Supreme VI
    b Elite Express
    c Supreme IV

13. **The Gardner 6LX engine first appeared in buses in:**
    a 1958
    b 1964
    c 1967

14. **When did England's last inland city tramway system close?:**
    a 1958
    b 1960
    c 1961

15. Which big bus fleet promoted itself in 1986 using the slogan 'Pick an orange'?:
- a Cardiff
- b Strathclyde
- c GM Buses

16. Bova coaches are made in:
- a Holland
- b Germany
- c Belgium

17. The approximate number of Ailsas built for service in Britain was:
- a 600
- b 800
- c 900

18. The Bristol Commercial Vehicles bus-building factory was closed in:
- a 1981
- b 1982
- c 1983

19. The last Fleetline chassis was sold to:
- a South Notts Bus Co
- b Southend Transport
- c Cleveland Transit

20. The last built-up Atlantean chassis was sold to:
- a Lancaster City Transport
- b Kuwait Transport Company
- c Merseyside Transport

◀ **21. This coach has bodywork by:**
- a Hestair Duple
- b Leyland
- c Jonckheere

22. This bus is operating in: ▶
- a Cardiff
- b Bristol
- c Exeter

◀ **23. This coach has bodywork by:**
- a Duple
- b Plaxton
- c ECW

Answers on page 125

24. This Routemaster belongs to: ▶
- a London Buses
- b Clydeside Scottish
- c Blackpool Transport

◀ **25. This parrot promoted public transport in:**
- a Paisley
- b Portsmouth
- c Grimsby

26. In which city was this Citybus logo used on buses?: ▶
- a Milton Keynes
- b Manchester
- c Belfast

Graham Wise

Cornwall independents before deregulation

The full effects of local bus service deregulation will take time to make themselves felt. Graham Wise looks at the activities of Cornwall's independents in the mid-1980s before deregulation took effect.

To mention Cornwall is to stir thoughts of holidays in an area of palm trees and sandy beaches, spectacular coastal scenery and the distinctive ruins of long-defunct copper and tin mines. To mention public transport in Cornwall is to stir thoughts of gleaming Great Western engines hauling chocolate and cream carriages, or the green buses of Western National. Times change and over the years things which seemed immortal have given way to new initiatives so that in some areas the once ubiquitous Western National bus is never seen at all. In their place have appeared a host of different coloured vehicles in the employ of numerous independent operators. Even the familiar green of Western National has given way to white, blue and yellow and the name is Cornwall Busways

Below:
This 1971 Willowbrook-bodied Bedford YRQ started life as a Bedford demonstrator. It was purchased by Grenville in 1975, having previously been owned by Blue Bus Services of Willington and then by Derby City Transport. It is seen in Falmouth in 1984.

and Coachways, although in East Cornwall and West Devon the old name still persists.

The rise of the independent came in the 1970s when Western National, in a period of severe cost-cutting, withdrew entirely from a number of areas in the county. These included Liskeard; northwest from Launceston to the coast — an area extending from Wadebridge in the south to the Devon boundary in the north and including the important centres of Tintagel and Bude; south and east of Truro from St Mawes almost to Mevagissey; the east side of the Lizard peninsula. In addition a number of individual routes was taken over by the independents as Western National closed services in other areas. The result is a wide mix of operators across the county with Western National still considered the main operator but with significant input from a range of undertakings who ensure that most areas have at least some access to public transport.

A glance at the independent operators' list in the front of the *Summer 1986 Cornwall Public Transport Timetable* reveals a total of 37 different firms of whom three were based over the border in Devon. A small proportion of the 34 Cornish operators comprises relatively large firms such as Grenville, Jennings and Fry's whilst the majority are small concerns with a few vehicles used on school or works' contracts and tours as well as on stage services. This means that most of the vehicles are coaches rather than buses thus providing a good standard of comfort for the rural passenger.

Above:
This unusual Marshall-bodied Bristol LHS6L was new in 1977 to Harvey of Mousehole. It is seen in its home town, about to depart for Penzance.

Population in Cornwall is located around a number of main centres — Penzance, Helston, Camborne-Redruth, Falmouth-Penryn, Truro, Newquay, St Austell, Padstow-Wadebridge, Bodmin, Bude, Liskeard, Launceston and Callington. These generate considerable amounts of traffic, especially on market days with some (such as Launceston) having thriving cattle markets as well. Whilst routes between main centres operate in many cases every weekday there is a large number of services geared to market-day and Saturday shopping. This means that many villages have only a limited service. Nevertheless, many of these have been instituted after careful planning by the operators and do provide a very convenient opportunity for visits to the main towns.

Above:
Even more unusual is this unique combination of Bristol LHS and Wadham Stringer Vanguard bodywork. This, too, belongs to Harvey and was new in 1981. It was photographed in Penzance in the summer of 1986.

The operators and their vehicles provide a fascinating kaleidoscope of activity although, superficially, there appear to be many similarities in outlook and presentation of the product. For a number of years up to summer 1986 almost all services were included in the County Council's Public Transport Timetable — also listed were trains, ferries and the Isles of Scilly helicopter link together with other airline services calling at St Mawgan. Sadly, after Deregulation it was not considered possible to continue this co-ordination although the intention is to revive the project as soon as practicable.

Several major operators are prominent on the scene. Mention has already been made of Grenville Motors Ltd of Troon near Camborne who also have a depot alongside the river at Penryn. Formed in 1947 the company has, over the years, absorbed several smaller operators and now serves important trunk routes from Camborne to Penzance, Camborne to Helston and Camborne to Falmouth, none of which duplicate Cornwall Busways services. There are also weekday town services in Camborne and daily ones in Falmouth/Penryn. Additionally there is a variety of routes operating on Fridays in and around Redruth. Whilst, like many others, Grenville's have made the Bedford chassis the mainstay of the fleet, they are noteworthy for the operation of many with Willowbrook bodywork most of which have bus seating and have been bought second-hand. Livery has traditionally been a drab dark red and cream but was changed in 1986 to white with orange trim.

In West Cornwall there are about five operators of whom the best known is probably Harvey of Mousehole (pronounced Mouzel!) with two buses running between Mousehole harbour and Penzance bus station alongside Cornwall Busways' Hoppas. The fleet in its blue and cream livery has recently comprised two Bristol LHS6Ls, one with Marshall bodywork which looks much the same back and front. The only Wadham Stringer Vanguard body on this chassis is fitted to the other. A third bus is kept in reserve in the shape of an ex-Halifax Joint Committee Albion Nimbus. In Penzance, K. Best

Above:
Truro out of season — note the Christmas lights — with a Plaxton-bodied Bedford YNT operated by Williams of St Agnes. It has Supreme VI bodywork, with shallow side windows.

trading as Mariner Coaches runs from the railway station forecourt to the heliport using a Plaxton-bodied Bedford midibus on a service taken over from British Airways. Other local services here are worked by Mounts Bay Coaches whose main concern is with tours and excursions, and Grenville with their Camborne route. Also in the area are Flora Motors of Helston with an interesting selection of buses (including ex-British Airways Atlanteans and an ex-City of Lincoln Panther) and coaches used on school contracts and a Thursdays and Saturdays route to Manaccan. Pollards and Runnals, both of Hayle, have several routes and contracts in this area and trade as Trelawney Tours and Primrose Coaches respectively.

Further east an important centre for independent operations is The Green at Truro. This is, in fact, a coach parking area almost opposite the Cornwall Busways garage on Lemon Quay. Here can be seen the vehicles of no less than seven operators with Wednesdays and Saturdays being the best days. Routes come in from Porthtowan, St Agnes, Perranporth, Newquay and St Mawgan in the north and St Mawes, Portscatho and Veryan in the south-east. The operators include Lidgey's Coaches of Tregony on the road to St Mawes, Tremain's Coaches of Zelah on the way to Newquay, Williams of St Agnes, Hopley of Mount Hawke, Liskey Tours of Perranporth, Harris of Summercourt and Roseland Motors of Veryan. Most of these operate at least one service on weekdays with Lidgey's and Tremain's providing the majority. Vehicles to be seen are mostly Bedfords with Duple or Plaxton bodywork — some are quite old and others quite new — including SBs (Roseland), a VAL70 (Hopleys) and a good number of Y-series. Of particular interest is a Seddon Pennine 6 with a Duple Viceroy body used by Harris of Summercourt.

Moving east, the St Austell and Bodmin area is the limit of Cornwall Busways operations, there being a considerable gap before reaching the Western National routes based on Plymouth which radiate out to Looe, Callington and Launceston. Interspersed with Cornwall Busways services around the two former towns are several independent services threading this

Above:
Pollard's Cherry Tree Coaches fleet includes this former London DMS, seen being steam cleaned at Western National's Camborne garage in 1983.

industrialised china-clay producing area. The St Austell district saw considerable population growth in the 1960s as the china-clay industry expanded, although bus services have not significantly increased as a result. Roselyn Coaches of Par and Cocks of Foxhole operate on Tuesdays, Thursdays and Fridays on routes into St Austell from Lerryn and Polgooth with Cocks' small fleet comprising mainly Fords. Also here are the familiar names of Roseland Motors, Lidgey's Coaches and Harris who have services on Fridays only with Harris's from Summercourt running only on the second and last Fridays each month. In the Bodmin area the main independent is H. G. Kinsman & Son Ltd who first introduced stage services in 1960, 10 years after the firm was founded. Eleven services are operated serving a variety of destinations including Plymouth, Trago Mills, Wadebridge and Lostwithiel. Confusingly there is also a service to a village called Withiel! Some of these run only on schooldays and the others only on specified days of the week. The fleet is a mixture of mainly Bedford and Ford but includes an ex-Alder Valley ECW-bodied Bristol RELL6L. All new purchases since 1964 have had registrations ending in 53.

North of Bodmin is the large area generally known as North Cornwall which includes Padstow, Wadebridge, Bude, Tintagel and Launceston. Apart from at Launceston, no Cornwall Busways vehicles are to be seen except for a few coaches on excursion work to the popular tourist spots. This is a large and thinly populated part of the county with no railways or improved roads: access tends to be difficult and slow. Within it there are about 11 operators with services finely tuned to meet the needs of a well-spread populace. Jennings of Bude have the largest number of routes and the largest fleet, the company being based at the old Western National garage in Lansdown Road, Bude, from which the NBC group withdrew in 1970. Town services are operated within Bude itself with times particularly geared to local schools' traffic and there are local services to Bideford (Tuesdays), Holsworthy (Wednesdays and Fridays) and to Marham, Widemouth and Poughill (Mondays to Saturdays). Most successful in recent years have been the express services to Plymouth and Exeter (Mondays to Saturdays), and Jennings modern coaches are a familiar sight in the bus stations of these two cities. The fleet is a modern one comprising mostly Duple or Plaxton-bodied Bedfords most of which have been purchased new.

Close behind Jennings in fleet strength is Fry's Bus Services of Tintagel. This little village

Above:
Roseland Motors operate this 1974 Bedford SB5 with Duple Dominant body. It was photographed at Tresillian on its way from Truro to Veryan in 1985.

Below:
Jennings operates a Bude town service; in August 1982 it was being run by this Plaxton-bodied Bedford YMT.

Left:
Fry's distinctive emblem.

attracts large numbers of holidaymakers and tourists, mostly because of its supposed links with King Arthur. Fry's are strategically located in the village centre from where they operate several stage services, school contracts and excursions. The fleet's notable feature is the medieval knight who appears on the sides of the vehicles — each one hand painted and a credit to the signwriter. Variety of vehicles is to be found in three Roe-bodied Panthers which came from Lincoln City Transport, a Harrington Grenadier-bodied AEC Reliance (ex-Greenslades) and a selection of the usual Bedfords and Fords with Duple and Plaxton coachwork. Services — all Mondays to Saturdays — are run to Bude, Launceston, Newquay and Plymouth, and one from Boscastle to Bude.

Other services in the area are provided by

Bottom:
Webber's local service in Liskeard in 1984, with a suitably signwritten Roe-bodied Leyland Panther. It was new to Lincoln City Transport in 1970.

Right:
A Ford of Gunnislake Volvo B58 picks up passengers at Calstock on its way to Tavistock. The bodywork is by Plaxton.

smaller undertakings such as Deeble, Guscott, Tilley's Coaches, Bruce and Roberts, and Launceston Car Hire in the Launceston area. Many of these only run on certain days of the week with a surge of activity on Tuesdays when there are cattle and general markets in Launceston. Guscott has a fleet of about 20 Bedfords, all second-hand, based at Halwill which is actually in Devon. Other interesting services are provided by Prout's Coaches of Port Isaac operating from there to Camelford on schooldays and to Wadebridge on Mondays, Tuesdays and Fridays, the Post Office Postbus on Mondays to Saturdays from Treburrick Letter Box — out in the middle of nowhere — to Wadebridge, and Barry Gill Motors of Wadebridge who provide services to suit college terms in their home town.

The final area to mention is that from opposite Fowey to Callington and including Liskeard. Webber's Travel of Blisland on Bodmin Moor is the main operator using ex-Lincoln Panthers, ex-Burnley and Pendle RESL6Ls and a good variety of mostly Leyland coaches — Leopards forming the backbone of the fleet. Services include Liskeard Town (with a specially painted Lincoln Panther), to Looe and to Plymouth on Mondays to Saturdays and a Blisland to Camelford schools service. Hambley of Pelynt near Looe has routes to Plymouth and Exeter; closely linked Deeble and Darley Ford Coaches also work into Liskeard and Clue's Coaches of Menheniot come into Liskeard on weekdays from the curiously named village of Doddycross. The latter's fleet is particularly interesting in being fairly elderly and including several Bedford SBs. Ford's Travel of Gunnislake have two services into Tavistock which serve villages in this remote part of the Tamar Valley using a mixture of Fords and Volvos. Their fleet also includes a couple of ex-East Kent AEC Regent Vs used on school contracts. Also in this area of small settlements and narrow lanes is Striplin of Tavistock who has a Friday service into that town from Stoke Climsland and a curious second-Thursday-in-each-month route from Lucket using Duple-bodied Bedfords.

As times move on so services must change and with Deregulation there are bound to be new developments. That is nothing new; over the years there has been continual change in Cornish bus services as operators have attempted to predict and meet changing travel patterns. What is certain is that the independent operator in Cornwall will continue to provide much of interest for the enthusiast and a reliable service for the traveller.

Right:
Treburrick letter box, with a Post Bus ready to leave for Wadebridge. It is an 11-seat Dodge 2000LB which was new in 1981.

Kevin Lane

Twixt Tyne and Wear

Photographer Kevin Lane illustrates some of the variety which could be found in the northeast of England in the early 1980s.

Above:
Neville Street, outside Newcastle Central Station, is a familiar location — but a 200mm lens gives it added impact. In this September 1981 view two Tyne & Wear PTE Metropolitans (both since withdrawn) share the evening rush-hour traffic with Atlanteans and a United Bristol VRT which was new to Western SMT.

Right:
The 08.00 Rapide to Liverpool loads at Newcastle's Gallowgate coach station in August 1985. The coach is a Northern General Leyland Royal Tiger Doyen.

Above:
Across the Tyne in Gateshead a Northern General Leyland Olympian arrives from Whitley Bay. In this 1985 view it was wearing Tyne & Wear's yellow and white livery, a practice abandoned during 1986.

Below:
Waiting to leave Chester-le-Street for Grange Villa in July 1982 is a former Cardiff AEC Swift in the General Omnibus fleet. It has a dual-doorway Alexander body. The service subsequently passed to Atkinson's Coaches.

Left:
The impressive viaduct which carries the East Coast main line over Durham provides a backdrop to this Northern General ECW-bodied Bristol RE coach in somewhat inappropriate all-over NBC poppy red bus livery. It is seen arriving from Flint Hill in July 1982.

Below:
Scarlet Band operate an hourly service between Ferryhill and Bowburn. This is Coxhoe, and a 1968 Plaxton-bodied Leyland Tiger Cub which was bought from Armstrong of Ebchester.

Left:
A Trimdon Motor Services Leyland Leopard with Duple body is joined by a United Leyland National at Sedgefield in 1981. The Leopard is bound for Hartlepool, the National for Middlesbrough. In 1981 United had two garages in the town but both are now closed.

Right:
Trimdon acquired a number of former NBC Bristol LHs in 1985, including this ECW-bodied bus which came from Devon General. It is seen in Sedgefield in September 1986.

Below:
Cleveland Transit vehicles gathered in Stockton High Street in October 1981. A lowheight Northern Counties-bodied Daimler Fleetline loads in front of Plaxton-bodied Leyland Leopards.

Bottom:
Middlesbrough Station bridge dictates the operation of a proportion of lowheight buses in the Cleveland fleet. On a damp and dismal day in June 1982 a Northern Counties-bodied Fleetline approaches the bridge.

John Milnes

Topless buses

'Off with their heads', said the Queen — a sentiment echoed by many generations of bus managers who have seen open-top buses as a way of creating more business. John Milnes shows some examples.

Left:
Perhaps the classic open-top bus: a half-cab double-decker in a seaside town. This is an ex-Southport Leyland Titan PD2 in the Merseyside fleet but still in its home town, and repainted in the red and cream Southport colours.

Below left:
At Rhyl on the North Wales coast Crosville operate open-top Daimler Fleetlines. This Northern Counties-bodied bus was new to Southdown and is named *Harlech Castle*. It is seen on the seafront at Rhyl.

Above:
Open-top buses have long been a feature of Essex resort Southend-on-Sea. Currently these are long-wheelbase Fleetlines with Northern Counties two-door bodies. Here one passes beneath the pier.

Below:
Open-top buses can be found inland as well — and few places are further from the sea in Britain than Sherwood Forest, where this ageing Lincolnshire Leyland Atlantean was photographed in 1984 on a service sponsored by Nottinghamshire County Council. This Atlantean was new in 1961 to Devon General and has bodywork by Metro-Cammell, built from the outset as a convertible open-topper.

Above:
Open-top buses have been used regularly on London sightseeing tours since the early 1970s. Present-day examples include Routemasters and a variety of former provincial buses such as this ex-West Yorkshire Road Car Bristol VRT with Eastern Coach Works body. It is operated by Cityrama and was photographed at the Tower.

Below:
Cardiff operates open-toppers on city tours. This is a Bristol VRT with an Alexander body, seen passing the Castle. The exact fare injunction seems incongruous on a leisure service.

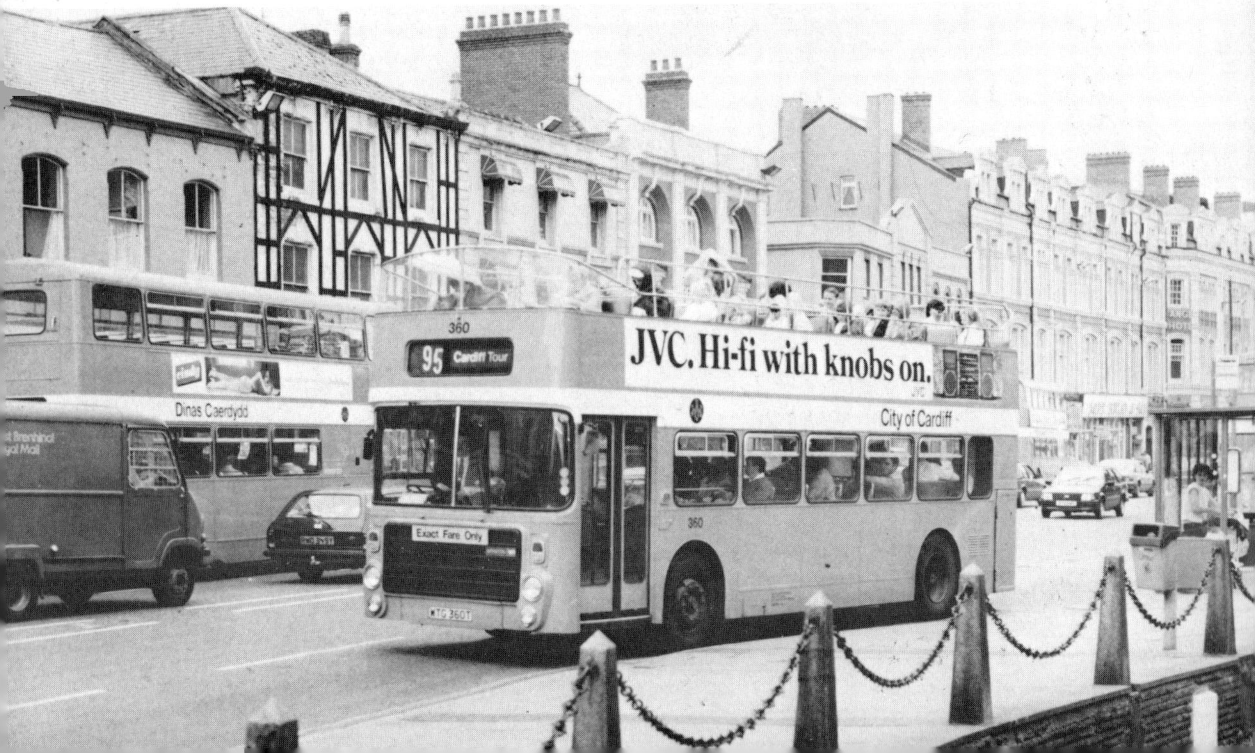

Geoff Mills

On hire to National

The mid-1980s saw a growing number of other operators' vehicles being painted in National Travel livery. Geoff Mills illustrates a selection.

Right:
This 1980 Plaxton-bodied Leyland Tiger of Premier Travel is seen in its home territory, Cambridge, after being repainted in National Express colours. However, it still retains a prominent Premier fleetname. The location is Drummer Street bus station.

Below right:
Unusual two-door Plaxton Supreme bodywork is fitted to this AEC Reliance operated by Hamilton of Yiewsley, West London. The coach was new in 1979 to Capital of Hayes. Note the non-standard application of the double-N logo at both ends of the National Express fleetname. It is seen leaving Colchester for London in the summer of 1986.

Above left:
A few Scottish Bus Group coaches wear National Holidays livery, as illustrated by this Midland Scottish Tiger with Duple Laser body. New in 1984, it is seen in St Malo, France, in 1986. Only the fleet number gives a clue to its ownership.

Top:
This 1982 Tiger of Nottingham City Transport has Duple Dominant IV bodywork. The registration number was originally carried by one of Nottingham's Daimler Fleetlines. It is seen leaving Peterborough for Lowestoft.

Above left:
Not quite what it seems, this is in fact a 1967 Leopard which was new to Wallace Arnold but was rebodied by Plaxton in 1979 for Allander Coaches of Milngavie, when it received its T-suffix registration. It is seen in the ownership of Tellyn Motor Services of Witham.

Left:
This Cityrama Berkhof-bodied DAF SB2300DHS is one of three operated in National Tourist Trail livery between London and Edinburgh. It is seen in Cambridge.

Top:
A number of Yelloway coaches are painted white including this 1979 Leopard with Plaxton body seen in Cardiff on its way to Rochdale, Yelloway's home town.

Above:
Bebb of Llantwit Fadre operate this Bedford Venturer with Duple Laser bodywork. It is seen in Colchester on the service from Cardiff.

Right:
One of the oddest vehicles to wear National Holidays livery is this Iveco 35-8 van with 12-seat coach conversion by Imperial Coachbuilders of Liverpool. It is operated by Newsome of Barnsley on feeder services to Dover.

Michael Dryhurst

The ones that got away

Pioneer bus preserver Michael Dryhurst looks at some of the important buses he would have liked to have seen preserved — but which were not.

There are now many hundreds, nay thousands, of public service vehicles preserved in the British Isles, and probably every major class of bus operated within the last 25 years is represented by those kept (hopefully) for posterity, along with many examples of less-common vehicles.

The preservation movement was for many years a very low-key affair, and those vehicles that were preserved were invariably the result of decision-making by an operator. The leader in this respect was London Transport and its predecessor, the London General Omnibus Co, and an example of all the major types operated by these concerns was preserved. The LGOC had kept a member bus each from the B, K and S classes, whilst the London Passenger Transport Board retained an NS, LT, ST and T. But they were not on show! Together with a couple of trams and a 1931 AEC trolleybus, these vehicles were kept for many years within the confines of Reigate garage, unseen by all those who would have appreciated them most. They did make occasional forays into the public gaze, such as the 25th Anniversary of the Omnibus Society in 1954 and the 1956 centenary parade of the LGOC in Regent's Park, London.

Below:
Among those that got away was this rare normal-control AEC Ranger. It survived until 1960.

A few, very few, provincial companies had preserved any of their buses and those that had could be counted on the fingers of one hand. Tram preservation also was in its infancy, being nurtured by the Light Railway and Tramway League. During the mid-1950s the forerunner of the National Bus Company, the British Transport Commission, assumed responsibility for the London Transport collection and started the moves toward a representative national collection of British public service vehicles, trams and trolleybuses. Individual purchase of withdrawn buses for the purpose of preservation was unknown.

In 1956, I made the acquaintance of Ken Blacker, Prince Marshall and Ron Lunn, all of whom had a profound influence on my life insomuch as here were three people who shared my intense interest in, and love of buses — their workings, design, routes — you name it, and our interest covered it. But these three friends were not satisfied with riding, looking at, listening to and photographing buses. They wanted to preserve one!

In 1929 the LGOC placed into service a number of the newly-introduced model 662 petrol-engined AEC Regals, on which was mounted a 31-seat rear-entrance LGOC-built body. Due to the intervention of World War 2, many of these buses survived longer than expected, even being rebuilt and re-engined in the late 1940s. But with the advent of the RF class AEC Regal IVs they were withdrawn from passenger service by 1953, and scrapped. Except one, T31. This bus, by now long-rebuilt with a forward entrance, had lasted as a driver-trainer but by mid-1956 had reached the end of its road and was to be withdrawn. Tentative enquiries were made to the London Transport Executive as to whether they would be prepared to sell the bus to a group of enthusiasts. And they were. But four of us was not enough, and John Cook, David Hurley, Alan Thomas and others were added, the reason for the consortium being so large was the fact that the price of T31 was £40, yes £40 0s 0d! As a Clapper Boy working at Pinewood Film Studios, my take-home pay was about £8 7s 6d (£8.35 to you); out of that came rent for the 'digs' in Ealing (well, Acton really, but Ealing Common was my nearest station . . .), fares to Uxbridge and Pinewood, meals, cinema visits, cigarettes (we all smoked in those days), etc etc, which at the end of the day, or rather the week, left about 10s (50p) for 'savings'. Don't ask me how, but somehow we cobbled together the necessary money and bought ourselves a 1929 AEC Regal I. But we learnt the hard way. Where would we keep it? Fortunately, Prince Marshall was friendly with a man who leased some open ground adjacent to Swiss Cottage tube station, and allowed us to park it there, but I will refrain from boring you further with the tribulations of being pioneer bus-preservationists. Suffice to say that we were bitten by the bug, and somehow we secured within two years a 1935 Gilford 168SD coach (one day I will bore you with an account of a trip to a Leyland rally in

Right:
This bus would have turned a few heads at a 1980s rally. A West Riding RT with centre-entrance Roe body in the red livery used for ex-tram routes.

Left:
Few Albion double-deckers have been preserved. Bedwas & Machen Urban District Council operated six buses in 1959 and this picture includes an Albion Venturer with Welsh Metal Industries body, with another just visible on the right.

this machine), a Leyland PLSC3 Lion and our first double-decker, CBC921, the Northern Counties-bodied AEC Renown which is now in the care of the Leicester Museums, this latter bus costing us the account-breaking sum of £85 0s 0d! But what about the heartbreaks, those buses that we could not afford to buy or keep and in which nobody else seemed interested?

Up in the far-flung outpost of Lincolnshire was the small independent operator Mr C. Barker, with the trading name of Grayscroft Coaches and working a stage service between Louth and Mabelthorpe. Among his dozen-odd fleet was a masterpiece, registered JN 8524, an AEC Ranger 665. This AEC model was basically a normal-control AEC Regal, and only a handful were built, but in 1937 the Tilling-BAT group subsidiary Westcliff-on-Sea Motor Services took delivery of some AEC coaches with Duple bodies, including some Rangers, which had 33-seat bodies built by the Hendon-based firm. In 1960 JN 8524 was the sole survivor of what was a most interesting (small) breed. We tried to raise the money to buy this magnificent vehicle, but our commitments precluded so doing; we did our best to attract other buyers, but without success. Nobody else seemed interested and the Ranger was scrapped. RIP.

I do not think that anyone (amongst those of us who can remember) would argue that the AEC Regent III was a classic bus. But why were so few (few? What am I talking about; only one is preserved!) of the 'provincial' RTs saved? AEC built about 60 of these in 1947, the chassis having the low-mounted RT-style radiator, engine and transmission, flanked by front wings as fitted to the previous model, the Regent II. Weymann bodied examples for Aberdeen, Devon General and South Wales, Roe supplied examples to Grimsby, Halifax and West Riding and two examples with Northern Counties bodies went to Douglas, Isle of Man, but I would venture to say that the best known buses of this type were the 15 delivered to Birmingham City Transport in 1947, which had standard Park Royal bodies modified to suit Birmingham practice. The last new AEC double-deckers received by Birmingham, these buses lasted well into the mid-1960s, but none was saved. Such a shame.

By 1958, the bus preservation movement was well under way. Earlier that year had been inaugurated the Vintage Passenger Vehicle Society under the guiding light of Ken Blacker, John Cook and Prince Marshall and myself. The Historic Commercial Vehicle Club had celebrated its organisation on a national scale with a rally at the Leyland works and the trade and enthusiasts publications carried articles about preservation, so that there was an awareness of and thus inspiration to preserve interesting old buses. Obviously, what qualified as such was a matter of individual taste.

Red and White Services Ltd, based at

Bulwark, Chepstow, had long favoured Albion chassis. It operated many other chassis types — including AEC, Bedford, Daimler, Guy, and Leyland — but the chassis synonymous with Red and White was Albion. After the war, the company took delivery of both double- and single-deckers from the Scottish vehicle builder, which at the time was still independent and not ensnared by the Leyland net. Examples of all these chassis types again lasted into the mid-1960s but failed to be saved, which is a double pity as so few Albion double-deckers are preserved, especially with Welsh bodywork. Both Red and White and the tiny municipal fleet of Bedwas and Machen Urban District Council had some Albions with lowbridge bodies by Welsh Metal Industries, one version of which was decidedly austere in looks but nonetheless well worthy of preservation. One must be thankful for memories, I suppose.

Because of the urgent need for buses and coaches in the period 1945-1950, there was a proliferation of smaller companies that entered into the manufacture of PSV bodywork or larger companies from other industries that decided to try their hand at building buses. One of the largest and happily still-surviving independent operators was Premier Travel of Cambridge, who in 1949 took delivery of three Daimler CV-series double-decker coaches with bodies of a somewhat old-fashioned look by the Leeds firm of Wilkes and Meade; these were of six-bay construction and had glass louvres over the windows. Again, survival into the 1960s, but no takers.

In the late 1950s and early 1960s, Gilbert's Coaches of Tunbridge Wells ran a number of vehicles almost equivalent to having their own permanent vintage vehicle rally, for in the summer of 1960 their fleet included a Dennis Lancet II with a dual-purpose body by Willowbrook, a Leyland Tiger TS7 with Harrington stepped-waist coachwork, and a 1939 Bedford WTB/Duple that had started life on the Isle of Wight. This latter vehicle passed into preservation, but I am not so sure about the Leyland, insomuch as in the current edition of *Preserved*

Below:
Probably the last traditional six-bay double-deckers were the three Daimlers in the Premier Travel fleet with Wilks & Meade coach bodies. They were new in 1950; all were scrapped.

Above:
Gilbert's Coaches of Tunbridge Wells owned this smart Harrington-bodied Leyland Tiger TS7 in 1961. It was new to North Western.

Vehicle Handbook by Keith Jenkinson it quotes an ex-North Western Road Car Co Tiger TS7 with a 1949 Windover body as being preserved, with registration JA 5514. This is the plate carried by the Gilbert's Coaches Leyland which I photographed at Regent's Park, London, in the summer of 1961, and I feel it unlikely that a body exchange took place. Despite having a photograph of it published in *Buses Illustrated*, Ken Blacker and I tried our utmost to obtain interest in the Dennis but to no avail, because apart from being a super vehicle it had benefited from the loving care that the proprietor lavished on the vehicles in this immaculate fleet.

Bearing in mind the large number of K5G Bristols that were put into service in the period 1937-39, I find it surprising that only a few survive in the preservation ranks, and only three remain with unaltered/unrebuilt bodywork. Particular favourites of the prewar Bristol K5G were those in the United Counties fleet which carried lowbridge bodies by Charles H. Roe of Leeds, a somewhat odd choice for a Tilling-BAT subsidiary company. Whilst the styling and general look of these buses was similar to their Eastern Coachworks counterparts, they were distinctly different. I well remember doing a day trip with Ken Blacker to Bedfordshire and Northants in the summer of 1958, and on finding a prewar Maudslay ML3 in service with Royal Blue Coaches of Pytchley we felt we had had our vehicle feast of the day until we saw this UCOC prewar K5G descending into Rushden and at the same time both realising it was bodied in Leeds, and not Lowestoft! I think most of this batch lasted until 1960 or possibly later, but again no one thought them of sufficient merit to warrant purchase for preservation and so another type disappeared into oblivion. If only half of the 120-odd postwar RTs preserved in Britain were kept and the owners of the other 60 had opted to preserve other types of buses from the provinces, oh, how different might it all have been . . .! What might they have bought instead of their RT?

Would it have been one of the Leyland Titan TD5 buses that Bournemouth Corporation bought in 1939? These magnificent buses were fitted originally with petrol engines whilst their luxuriously-appointed Weymann bodies featured a sliding portion in the roof, full-front cab, and in addition to the normal rear platform and staircase they boasted front stairs with a forward exit and folding doors. These buses always had a great appeal to me, especially as they had much in common with the 21 AEC Regents delivered to Brighton Corporation at about the same time, particularly in styling, and in having Alhambrinal-lined ceilings. The Bournemouth buses received oil engines in the postwar period and were a familiar sight in the (then) Hampshire resort until the early 1960s, when some were converted to open-top configuration. One survives in this latter form but, unfortunately, not so any of the original batch.

I am not sure which is worse. Not to have been preserved at all and scrapped, or to have been saved and subsequently broken-up. In 1937, Leyland Motors supplied to London Transport 100 of their Titan TD4, of which 90 were fitted with standard crash gearbox, whilst the remainder sported torque-convertors making

Above:
At the same time Gilbert's fleet included this prewar Dennis Lancet II with Willowbrook body. It is seen in Hove in 1960.

Below:
This Roe-bodied Bristol K5G was still in service with United Counties almost 25 years after being built — but it escaped preservation.

them more akin to the fluid transmission STL-type AEC, which was the London standard of the time. The bodies on these buses were built by Leyland also, whereby the standard Leyland design was modified to conform to LPTB practice, thus resembling the STL but being undeniably a product of Lancashire rather than Middlesex. The type spent the greater part of its London career at Hendon garage but with the advance of the RT programme they were reallocated to Ponders End, where they displaced Guy wartime austerity buses. The class stayed intact until 1954 and was then sold, with most of the vehicles going for scrap, but in 1958 Ken Blacker and I tracked down one in Leamington Spa, with Priory Coaches. We went up to see it and it was in good condition, the only disappointment being that it had lost its roof route number box, but this could have been replaced.

At the time I had just bought the ex-Leicester Renown (good that I bought it, eh?), Ken had a Leyland Lion PLSC3 and was after the little Thornycroft bus from Tiffin School, and Prince Marshall was up to his eyes in Gilfords, so none of us had funds, although we were determined that this one would not slip through the net. We had recently formed The Vintage Passenger Vehicle Society and a member, on reading of the bus in our news sheet, expressed great interest in the bus and bought it. In time, STD90 was brought down to the pottery in White Hart

Top:
Another escapee from the ranks of preserved buses . . . a 1939 Bournemouth TD5 with full-front, forward exit and sliding roof. This is a 1958 photograph.

Right:
The author's first double-decker was this ex-Leicester Renown, seen at a rally at the AEC factory in 1958. The late Prince Marshall, an active preserver of old buses, stands by the front wing.

Lane, Tottenham, where we parked our vehicles, and took its place in the VPVS 'fleet'. One day about a year later, Ken and I went to the pottery in order to get the Renown ready for a rally (yes, even 28 years ago there were bus rallies!), and the STD wasn't there, conspicuous by its absence, and it was never to return. The owner had lost interest, and without soliciting any of the group, had sold the bus for scrap . . .

Obviously, all of us have different ideas and thoughts about what does, and what doesn't, qualify for preservation. At the time of writing I own three buses — EYK 396, the 1948 RT that carries the 1938 RT1 body and is known by that number, FUF 63, a 1939 AEC with Weymann body, and VLT 254, a Routemaster in which I am a part-owner. Although I am an avid AEC fan, my interest is wider, having just disposed of a Bristol LDS6B Lodekka, and there are a number of other buses that I would have liked to have owned, if only to prevent their demise, such as one of the Maidstone and District Leyland TD5s of 1939, which were supplied new with open-top bodies by Weymann and because of their limited use lasted well into the 1960s. Birch Bros was a well-liked company, with an impressive fleet that relieved the monotony of London Transport buses on the streets of the capital. Their handsome double-deckers, such a familiar sight on the road from King's Cross to Rushden, would have been very welcome in my collection. These had Willowbrook bodies, there being two batches, one mounted on the Guy Arab III and the rest on Leyland Tiger PS1 (yes, both types were on single-decker chassis).

Minor coachbuilders such as Welsh Metal Industries, Santus and Scottish Aviation bodied Foden double-deckers, but I would have been just as happy with one of the Brush-bodied versions that Derby Corporation had. Another bus that sold in huge numbers was the Daimler COG5, but so few complete double-deckers of this type exist. What a great pity that nobody saw fit to preserve the 1939 COG5 with all-metal Northern Counties body which was used by the Stalybridge, Hyde, Mossley and Dukinfield Joint Transport and Electricity Board as a driver trainer until 1963/64. And is anyone going to grab one of the Southdown Leyland Titan PD3 'Queen Marys' before they all disappear? And I don't mean the 1964 convertibles which are mostly still in service or the later version kept by the British Shoe Corporation; I'm talking about a VUF/XUF/CD-registered bus. You know, the familiar ones.

But, on the other hand, all of us enthusiasts must be grateful for the fantastic array of passenger-carrying vehicles that has been saved, and those who take on trolleybuses and trams deserve a medal!

Below:
This Birch Leyland Tiger with Willowbrook body is representative of the company's double-deck coaches. None were preserved.

Simon Butler

Over and under

Simon Butler illustrates a selection of buses passing under or crossing over bridges in various parts of England.

Right:
A pair of Reading Transport double-deckers illustrate the gradient on the bridge over the River Kennett in Duke Street, in the town centre. Leading is one of two Leyland Titans delivered in 1979; behind is an MCW Metropolitan. Both models had short production lives and Reading now buys Leyland Olympians.

Below:
A narrow bridge at Moreton, Essex, with a London Country Leyland National bound for Ongar. This route was previously operated by Eastern National, passing to London Country in 1984.

LENL971
MMB971P

Above right:
A threatening storm provides a backdrop to a Crosville Leyland National in dual-purpose livery on the bridge over the railway outside Crewe station in the summer of 1985.

Right:
A bridge from the northeast is an obligatory item for inclusion on any photo-feature based on bridges. This grand structure is at Sunderland. The bus is a Northern General ECW-bodied Leyland Olympian. JTY 390X

Below:
Safeguard of Guildford operate this 1982 Leyland Leopard with Duple Dominant bus body. It is seen passing under the railway line from Effingham Junction to Waterloo in 1983.

Above right:
Not quite a bridge, more a ramp. This is the approach to Terminal 1 at Heathrow Airport with an Alder Valley Tiger climbing up to the departure area. It has a Plaxton Paramount 3500 body.

Right:
Bridges abound in the area of Waterloo station. A London Transport AEC Merlin pauses in Waterloo Road while on a Red Arrow service in 1981.

Below:
Perhaps the most famous bridge of all — London's Tower Bridge with a short-lived Metropolitan heading north for Shoreditch in 1980.

Sandy Macdonald

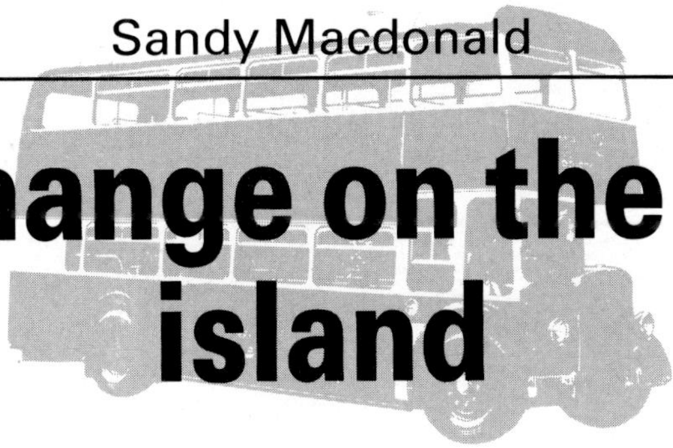

All change on the long island

Buses Scottish columnist, Sandy Macdonald, documents developments in the Western Isles — an interesting area off the beaten bus-enthusiast track.

The 130-mile-long strip of islands and islets about 40 miles off the northwest coast of Scotland and stretching from the Butt of Lewis in the north to Barra Head in the south are collectively called the Western Isles, the Outer Hebrides, the Outer Isles or simply the Long Island. These islands can be reached by air services from Glasgow or Inverness and by ferries from Oban, Skye or Ullapool, and have a total population of less than 40,000. Crofting, fishing, weaving and tourism are the main traditional industries and the only real town is Stornoway which is the administrative capital. It is situated on the largest and most northerly island of the group, part of which is called Lewis and the remainder Harris. It is on this island that most public transport interest is to be found, but others of interest from this point of view are North Uist, Benbecula and South Uist which are linked by a series of causeways and bridges, and Barra.

Up to the end of the 1970s there was relative stability in the provision of bus services on the Long Island. At that time Lewis and Harris had a fairly comprehensive network of services provided by a number of operators, the largest of which was John Mitchell of Stornoway, also trading as Western Lewis Coaches. This operator first ran buses in 1920 and during the

Below:
These Willowbrook-bodied Bedford SB5s were new to Mitchell of Stornoway. In 1986 they were photographed in the ownership of MacDonald of Back (right) and Lochs Motors (left).

1930s and 1940s expanded by acquiring many smaller businesses all over the island. In 1979, the dark blue and cream buses provided services within Stornoway and from that town to Carloway, Ness, North Tolsta and Back. Another well-established company was Stornoway-based Hebridean Transport, formed after World War 2 by the amalgamation of a number of smaller operators on the Eye Peninsula of Lewis. The red, maroon and cream buses in this fleet linked Stornoway to the crofting townships of Melbost, Swordale, Bayble and Portnaguran on that peninsula. Other companies running into Stornoway were Galson-Stornoway Motor Services which shared the route between Stornoway and Ness with Mitchell; Lochs Motor Transport with a route to Ranish; J. A. MacLennan of Stornoway with a weekly service to Breanish; Harris Garage Co Ltd of Tarbert (Harris) with a service to Tarbert taken over from Highland Omnibuses in 1975 when that company withdrew from the Western Isles; Murdo Kennedy with a run to South Lochs and Orinsay; and the Post Office Corporation with a route to Callanish and Timsgarry. On the other islands several postbus services operated on North Uist, Benbecula and Barra, but the only other operators of stage carriage services were MacAuley Brothers of Lochboisdale in South Uist with routes between Lochboisdale, Ludag and Benbecula Airport, and A. Macintyre of Grean, Barra, with a service between Castlebay and Eoligarry.

In addition to the provision of local services, another important use for buses in such rural areas is the transport of school children. Several other companies were involved in this type of work and the local authority, Western Isles

Above:
This smart Duple Dominant bus-bodied Bedford is regularly used by Harris Garage on the main service between Stornoway and Harris.

Left:
Not quite what it seems, this ECW-bodied bus owned by Dodson is in fact a *Ford*. It was new to Hants & Dorset.

Council, also maintained a small fleet of buses smartly painted black and white for school services and other council work. The islands could therefore boast not less than 20 bus operators in the late 1970s.

During the 1980s there have been quite a few changes to this picture. The biggest upheaval occurred right at the beginning of the decade when the nine-route network of Mitchell/ Western Lewis Coaches was abandoned after a protracted dispute with the Western Isles Council over subsidies and a concession fare scheme. The terms of subsidy offered to Mitchell by the Council had not been acceptable to the operator and during 1979 an ultimatum was given to the Council by Mitchell. As this did not work, new contractors had to be found to operate the services from 1 January 1980. The Stornoway town services passed to Lochs Motor Transport together with the West Side circular route linking Stornoway to Carloway and other settlements on the west coast of Lewis. The services from Stornoway to Back and North Tolsta were taken over by MacDonald of Back, and the Stornoway-Ness journeys were incorporated into the existing operations on the same route of Galson-Stornoway Motor Services. Mitchell continued to run contract services for the Arnish oil rig construction yard near Stornoway but with all the stage carriage work gone most of the fleet was redundant. Although in earlier years the Mitchell fleet contained quite a bit of variety including an ex-Aberdeen Corporation Guy Wolf toastrack and a Bedford VAL service bus, the standard vehicle had latterly been the Duple or Willowbrook-bodied Bedford SB service bus complete with the unusual feature of a wooden slatted rear seat, to minimise vandalism. One such vehicle was

Above:
Among other ex-NBC Fords in the Hebrides is this Duple-bodied example owned by McIver and seen at Garrabost in 1986. It was new to United Counties.

retained by Mitchell, together with a pair of recently delivered Bedford SB5s with military-style Marshall bodies, for use on the contract work. Mitchell finally gave up bus operation at the end of 1983 to concentrate on the Bedford/ Vauxhall dealership side of the business.

No sooner had services settled down again than news of another major change became public. In the early part of 1981 the directors of Hebridean Transport decided to sell the business and a new owner was soon found in D. H. M. McIver and Sons Ltd, also of Stornoway. By June of that year McIver had taken over operation of the services and all the Hebridean Transport vehicles, although interest was added immediately by the purchase of four ex-United Counties Duple Dominant-bodied Ford R1014 buses and three new Duple-bodied Bedford YMT coaches. The Hebridean Transport fleetname was retained by the new owner but a new livery of white and blue was adopted. Another development by McIver was the introduction of an express service between the mainland terminal of the Caledonian Macbrayne Stornoway/Ullapool ferry and Glasgow, with connections provided from there to Edinburgh. Two of the new coaches were based on the mainland for this summer-only service which only lasted two seasons.

Many other changes have also taken place during the 1980s. At the beginning of 1980 the Garbutt business on Benbecula was given up, after which Buchanan Brothers of Liniclete started up and have continued the operation of school contract work there until the present

Above:
The largest school in Lewis, the Nicholson Institute, is a major focus of bus activity. From left to right can be seen vehicles of MacDonald of Balallan, Lochs Motor Transport, and the Western Isles Council.

time. Amongst the vehicles run latterly by Garbutt were a trio of ex-Southern Vectis Bedford SB8 coaches and an ex-Highland Omnibuses Park Royal-bodied AEC Reliance. In Lewis the MacLennan Uig and Bernera service was given up in the spring of 1980, passing to Dodson, also of Stornoway. The only vehicle owned by MacLennan was a Duple-bodied Ford Thames Trader, previously with Galson-Stornoway Motors but new to Trimdon Motor Services. After only one year of operating it, Lochs Motor Transport gave up the Stornoway-Carloway route to MacKay of Dalbeg in 1981, thus introducing another new stage carriage operator to Stornoway. Another development about this time was the commencement of a couple of local minibus services on Benbecula and the north end of South Uist by a community-based organisation with the Gaelic title of Co-Chomunn an Iochdair Ltd and based at Eochar, South Uist. In the summer of 1986 the services of MacAuley Brothers of Lochboisdale were taken over by MacDonald of Howmore, with MacAuley continuing in business as a haulage contractor. Up to the end of 1971 the MacAuley services had been operated by David MacBrayne Ltd, and when the licences changed hands at that time they were accompanied by three Duple Midland-bodied Bedford VAS1 buses. Further former MacBrayne Bedfords were added to the MacAuley fleet during the 1970s. All the buses owned by MacAuley passed to Macdonald's Hebridean Coaches fleet in 1986 and included four ex-Highland Scottish Ford buses with Alexander or Willowbrook bodies.

The 1985 Transport Act has brought about further significant changes in the area, especially in Lewis. Taking advantage of the new freer atmosphere for starting local services, Murdo Macleod of Tong near Stornoway, trading as Moley's Minicoaches, began a service in September 1986 between Stornoway and Tong via Benside. This service provided competition for Lochs Motors' Newmarket route and the North Tolsta, Back and Tong services of MacDonald.

As might be expected, no services in the Western Isles were registered as commercial by any operator and consequently all routes were put out to tender by the Western Isles Council. This exercise was completed in time for Deregulation Day on 26 October 1986 and resulted in the award of local service contracts to the existing operators, with a few significant exceptions. Firstly, the Stornoway-Carloway service changed hands for the third time in six years as Lochs Motor Transport outbid MacKay for the route, leaving that company with only school contract work. Secondly, Lochs also won the contract to provide all the services previously operated by McIver between Stornoway, Swordale, Bayble and Portnaguran. Thirdly, the Council decided not to provide a subsidy to Moley's Minicoaches but to include Benside in the package of routes for which Lochs Motors had successfully tendered. These decisions removed MacKay and McIver from local service operations subsidised by the Council with most of McIver's dozen buses being rendered redundant. However, McIver declared their intention to compete with Lochs without subsidy not only on those routes which had been lost but also on services within Stornoway.

With such a variety of operators, vehicle interest has remained high throughout this period, although most are lightweight types. One fleet containing both lightweight and heavyweight machines is Lochs Motors, including a pair of ex-Hutchison, Overtown Willowbrook-bodied AEC Reliances, a pair of

Left:
MacDonald of Back operates a pair of ex-Eastern Scottish Bedfords with Alexander bodywork.

ex-Mitchell Bedford SB5/Willowbrook buses, three ex-South Wales Ford R1014/Willowbrook buses and several Duple-bodied Ford coaches. All of these vehicles are in a red and white livery but when the additional contracts were won in 1986 four Duple Dominant bodied Fords were bought from Midland Scottish, and as some had been freshly painted cream and blue by their previous owner, the decision was taken to keep them in that livery for use on the ex-McIver routes.

Another company which has over the years contained a wide variety of vehicle types is Galson-Stornoway Motor Services. The mid-1980s' fleet contains several Plaxton-bodied Leyland Leopard coaches and several Bedfords with a variety of coachwork. A maroon, cream and red livery has recently been adopted and in 1986 fleet numbers began to appear on vehicles. The only other operator in the area to use fleet

Below:
Few Marshall-bodied Bedford SB5s are to be found in psv service. This is one of a pair which were new to Mitchell but were subsequently purchased by McIver.

numbers is MacDonald of Back and this, together with a smart green and red livery and the consistent use of destination screens, gives a very good impression of the fleet. Buses currently owned include one of the ubiquitous ex-Mitchell Willowbrook-bodied Bedfords, two similar vehicles which were new to MacBrayne, two ex-Eastern Scottish Alexander-bodied Bedford YRTs and a pair of Duple Dominant-bodied Ford R1014 buses. Two Duple-bodied Bedford coaches also owned are painted in brown and cream coach colours.

Although a couple of coaches are owned, Dodson's service has been maintained for the past few years by a pair of Eastern Coach Works-bodied Ford R1014s new to Hants and Dorset, still in poppy red but with 'Uig and Bernera Service' inscribed above the windows. The maroon and grey vehicles of Harris Garage were decorated with a hand-painted map of the Western Isles until a few years ago but some interesting vehicles are still owned, including a Duple Dominant bus-bodied Bedford YLQ and a Plaxton-bodied Bedford VAS5, both bought new.

Even the smaller companies which do not operate local services manage to provide vehicle interest. A classic example must surely be MacDonald of Balallan, for many years the owner of an ex-demonstration Marshall-bodied Dodge S307 which was tried by several operators in the 1960s. Although still owned, this unique bus is now out of use, the current operational fleet consisting of an ex-Mitchell Bedford SB5/Willowbrook and an ex-City of Oxford Duple Dominant bus-bodied Ford R1014. Fleet livery is blue and white. In the Uists, both MacCuish and MacDonald of West Gernish recently added a 7ft 6in-wide ex-West Coast Motors Duple-bodied Bedford SB5 to their fleets, while the Buchanan fleet contains an ex-Irvine of Salsburgh AEC Reliance with Plaxton bus body, an ex-Highland Scottish Ford R192 with Willowbrook body and a similar Ford R1014 new to City of Oxford.

It can be seen from the foregoing that many of the bus operators in these islands are continuing what has been a strong tradition of using purpose-built service buses, and consequently the level of interest in the area is considerable. The Western Isles Council has recently, very thoughtfully, built a new bus station at South Beach, Stornoway, to replace the previous stances at South Beach and Bayhead, making it easier to see vehicles of many of the operators already mentioned. It is recommended that any readers who have not yet ventured to the Western Isles should do so at the first opportunity.

Below:
Lochs Motor Transport owns this pair of ex-South Wales Ford R1014s. They have Willowbrook bodies.

Reg Wilson

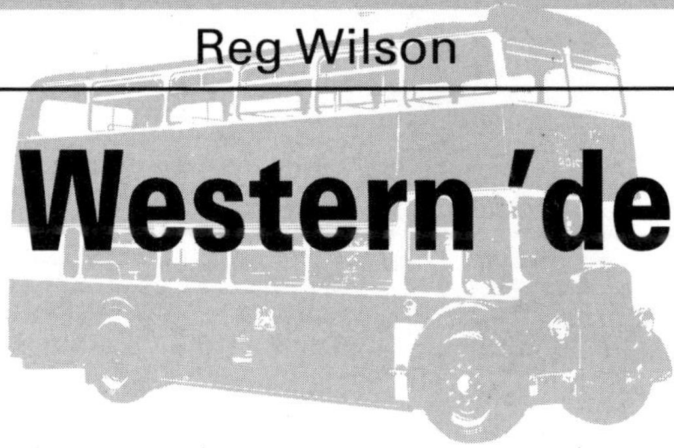

North Western 'deckers

After an absence of some 15 years the name North Western was revived in 1986 for a new NBC subsidiary in Merseyside. Reg Wilson illustrates a selection of old and new North Western double-deckers.

Right:
The Bristol K typifies North Western's double-deckers of the late prewar period. This is a 1938 K5G with lowbridge ECW bodywork which when new had seats for a mere 47 passengers. Note the six-bay construction. It was photographed in Manchester in 1950, shortly before being rebodied by Willowbrook.

Below right:
A less typical North Western Bristol, this is a 1942 K5G with Strachan body which was acquired from Potteries Motor Traction in exchange for a non-standard Daimler CWG5. It joined the North Western fleet in 1947 and in 1953 was fitted with the ECW body displaced from a rebodied prewar K5G of the type illustrated in the previous photograph. It was sold in 1956.

Right:
Few prewar Titans were operated by North Western. One was this 1939 TD5 with Leyland body which was purchased from Corless of Coppull in 1947. It ran until 1954.

Below right:
Postwar Titans were commonplace. This is one of 10 Weymann-bodied PD2/1s which entered service in 1949 and ran until 1966. Perhaps prophetically, it was photographed in Liverpool, a major target for the post-1986 North Western company.

Below:
The only North Western Titans with new-look fronts were 10 PD2/21s delivered in 1956. Weymann built the lowbridge bodywork which was fitted with doors on the rear platform. These buses were North Western's last lowbridge 'deckers and were sold in 1971; this one is seen when new.

Bottom right:
The company's first lowheight 'decker was this 1960 Dennis Loline with Gardner 6LX engine and forward-entrance East Lancs bodywork. It was one of 15 Lolines of which three were Gardner-powered while the remainder had Leyland engines. In this 1972 view it is seen in the ownership of Selnec (Cheshire), after the break-up of North Western.

Right:
The company's most stylish buses were Alexander-bodied Daimler Fleetlines. It bought 95 between 1963 and 1967. This was one of the first batch, delivered in 1963 and photographed when new.

Below right:
As well as buying Fleetlines, North Western bought AEC Renowns in 1963 and 1964. These had Park Royal bodywork. This is a view of Wilmslow depot in December 1971, three days before the Selnec takeover.

Below:
The first Bristol double-deckers to be ordered by North Western since the long-lived prewar Ks were 25 VRTs. These, however, were built after the takeover of part of the company's operations by the Selnec PTE and were delivered direct to the PTE in 1973. This one is seen in Stockport in 1977, in the ownership of Greater Manchester Transport. These 75-seaters could carry 43 passengers in their upper saloons — only four less than the *total* capacity of a prewar K.

Bottom right:
North Western rides again. In September 1986 the North Western name was revived for the Bootle-based company formed to take over the southern half of Ribble's operations. The new company adopted a red and blue livery, with the colours divided by a diagonal white stripe. This ECW-bodied Leyland Olympian was one of the first ex-Ribble buses to be repainted and was photographed in Ormskirk.

Michael Fowler

Channel Isle

Michael Fowler visited Guernsey in 1986 where operations are largely in the hands of Trafalgar subsidiary Guernseybus — but with an interesting variety of vehicles.

Above:
A line-up at the St Peter Port bus terminus captures the spirit of Guernsey's bus operations in the 1980s. Flanked by a pair of ex-London Transport Bristol LHs are two Bedford J4 truck chassis with incredibly old-fashioned bodywork by Reading (on the right) and Sparshatt (on the left) which belies the fact that these buses were built in 1968 and 1972 respectively.

Right:
The last of the old-style Sparshatt bodies were delivered in 1972; the design dated back to the mid-1950s. This is a 1972 Bedford J4 with the rear of a sister vehicle visible in the background, complete with centrally-located rear emergency door. These buses are 34 seaters.

Above right:
In 1974 a batch of Bedford J6s was delivered with Seddon bodywork, a rare combination indeed. There are four buses of this type. This one is seen leaving Cobo Bay for St Peter Port.

Right:
The next new buses were Bedford SB5s with Wadham Stringer bodywork, of which there are 10. The high-set body emphasises the vehicle's narrow width. The A prefix to the fleet number identifies vehicles less than 7ft 4in wide and which can use any roads on the island.

Below:
There is a pleasant irony in the advert on the side of this ex-London Transport ECW-bodied Bristol LH advertising flights to its former operating territory.

Above:
Not all of the Bristol LHs acquired by Guernseybus have had ECW bodywork. Unusual Marshall bodywork is fitted to this LHS6L which was new to Devon General in 1972. It is seen passing the airport.

Below:
This narrow Bristol LH6L was new in 1975 to NBC subsidiary Greenslades of Exeter. It has a 7ft 6in wide Plaxton Panorama Elite 45-seat body and is seen on an excursion at the Little Chapel.

Above:
The 'Discover Old Guernsey Tour' is operated by Island Coachways using this singularly appropriate coach — a 1948 Austin CXB with 33-seat Barnard body complete with sliding sun roof, a feature calculated to create apoplexy in modern safety legislators. It was new to Guernsey Motors.

Right:
The modern Island Coachways fleet also has interesting vehicles — such as this 1973 Bedford SB with a Duple Dominant body which has been reduced in width from 8ft 2½in to 7ft 4in by slicing a piece out of the centre.

Below right:
Ford's new Transit, launched at the beginning of 1986, was quick to appear on Guernsey as shown by this vehicle in Trafalgar's corporate colours photographed in August.

Quiz answers

1 b	**10** a	**19** a
2 b	**11** b	**20** b
3 a	**12** a	**21** a
4 c	**13** a	**22** b
5 a	**14** b	**23** a
6 a	**15** a	**24** c
7 c	**16** a	**25** c
8 a	**17** a	**26** a
9 c	**18** c	

Robert Grieves

Scotland in winter

Varied views of the frozen — and sometimes unfrozen — north from the collection of Robert Grieves.

Right:
'Dreich' is how a Scot would sum-up this atmospheric view of a wet winter's day in Banff. The bus is a German-built Argus, operated between Banff and Macduff by Horne's Motor Services.

Below:
Harper of Blairgowrie ran this 1929 Model A Ford to remote Enochdu in Perthshire. Harper had a mail contract and his bus is seen here struggling in the snow while delivering the mail.

Below right:
The main road from Perth to Pitlochry in the early 1930s is the setting for this AEC Reliance of the Pitlochry Motor Co, marooned complete with passengers when the River Tummell burst its banks. It had a Hall Lewis body.

Right:
In the winter of 1936 an Alexander Leyland Tiger TS7 pauses at Tyndrum on its way from Oban to Glasgow. The radiator blind is supplemented by a newspaper in an effort to maintain a reasonable water temperature.

Below:
Willing hands help clear snow for this Bedford OB of Leask of Lerwick in the Shetland Isles. It is on service from Lerwick to Toft.

Bottom:
Woolly hats and scarves are much in evidence in this 1962 view of a 1948 Roe-bodied Crossley on the service to Lanark operated by Jackson of Auchenheath. The Crossley was ex-Edinburgh Corporation. This was the last year of operation by Jackson.

Right:
A Massey-bodied Daimler CVG6 in the fleet of McGill's of Barrhead pauses in the slush in central Paisley in 1966 while on its way to Renfrew.

Below:
Melting winter snows flooded the road near Bargrennan, between Newton Stewart and Ayr, when this Alexander-bodied Leyland Leopard of Western SMT was photographed creating waves in 1978.

Bottom:
A pretty picture — but not one that would be appreciated by the drivers who had to start and drive the frozen Fleetlines parked outside Western SMT's Inchinnan depot in January 1980.